These Will Preach!

Stories And Metaphors
For The Pulpit

Jerry Schmalenberger

CSS Publishing Company, Inc., Lima, Ohio

THESE WILL PREACH!

Scripture quotations are from the *New Revised Standard Version of the Bible*, copyright 1989 by the Division of Christian Education of the National Council of the Churches of Christ in the USA. Used by permission.

Library of Congress Cataloging-in-Publication Data

Schmalenberger, Jerry L.
    These will preach : stories and metaphors for the pulpit / Jerry Schmalenberger.
        p.   cm.
    ISBN 0-7880-1326-2 (pbk.)
    1. Homiletical illustrations. 2. Lutherans—Anecdotes. I. Title.
BV4225.2.S35   1999
251'.081—dc21   98-44908
                                                                                      CIP

This book is available in the following formats, listed by ISBN:
    0-7880-1326-2   Book
    0-7880-1327-0   Disk
    0-7880-1328-9   Sermon Prep

PRINTED IN U.S.A.

Dedication

This collection of preaching resources is dedicated to the students, staff, and faculty of the Augustana-Hochschule in the little Bavarian village of Neuendettelsau, Germany. Here I have spent a Franconian sabbatical after retirement as President of Pacific Lutheran Theological Seminary in Berkeley, California.

In the midst of this village of mercy and mission permeated with the nineteenth century spirit of Wilhelm Loehe, I have had the luxury of composition, worship, friendship, and reflection on 36 years of preaching.

May this sacred seed-bed of "the called" always be blessed with God's special presence.

JLS

The title of this book is an answer to a question often asked of me by friend and President of the Graduate Theological Union, Glenn Bucher. When I would relate a story to him, he would ask, "Will it preach?" Yes, Glenn, *These Will Preach!*

Table Of Contents

Introduction

I have written this collection of metaphors, narratives, and observations for use by preachers who already know the power of narrative preaching.

In my book, *The Preacher's Edge*,[1] I encourage "close to the ground preaching" which uses the extended narrative or analogy or metaphor. I also recommend the use of a homiletical journal in which the preacher records stories, experiences, and observations which one day might be usable for this style of preaching.

David Buttrick claims in his book *Homiletic*,[2] "Preaching reaches for metaphysical language because God is a mysterious presence-in-absence. God is not an object in view. Therefore, preaching must resort to analogy, saying, 'God is like....' The language of analogy is profoundly related to fields of lived experience."

Charles E. Miller writes: "Jesus loved analogies and metaphors. That is why he asked himself while preparing to preach, 'What is the kingdom of heaven like? To what shall I compare it?' Analogy is based on the principle that we proceed from the known to the unknown. It points out the similarities between what is already understood, appreciated, persuasive or evident and what is not."[3]

To this end, I provide these possibilities for metaphors and analogies I have collected in my homiletical journals over my many years of ministry in parish and seminary.

They are not from sermon illustration books, but from my own life experiences, observations, and deep feelings of the heart.

There are quite a number of televison commercials included because I know millions of dollars go into researching what reaches and moves people before a commercial is ready for showing. We can use the benefits of this expertise in our preaching and touch our people as well.

After writing out all these observations from my little pocket journals I carried, I tried to put them in categories which may prove helpful.

It is my hope that not only will this collection serve as a resource for you in extended metaphor and narrative preaching, but that it will also motivate you to make your own collection. For surely your own will be much more effective than those I have gathered for my use.

In his book *Telling the Story*,[4] Richard Jensen says: "Biblical text should be meditated on the light of stories we know from literature, theater, movies, television, and so forth. This is called vertical exegesis. It thinks about a given text in relation to other stories which you know. This aspect of vertical exegesis does its homework in pastoral calling and visitation. There are living stories all around you. Surely the best preaching we do is that preaching where text (horizontal exegesis) and people (vertical exegesis) meet in creative encounter."

Help yourself to what my heart has said to me would be valuable, and consider your own collection as well.

Jerry L. Schmalenberger

1. Jerry L. Schmalenberger, *The Preacher's Edge* (Lima, Ohio: CSS Publishing Co., 1996).

2. David Buttrick, *Homiletic* (Philadelphia: Fortress Press, 1987), p. 116.

3. Charles E. Miller, C.M., *Ordained to Preach* (New York: Alba House, 1992), p. 41.

4. Richard Jensen, *Telling the Story* (Minneapolis: Augsburg-Fortress Press, 1980), p. 158.

Alive In Christ
Dave Carlson of Iowa Lutheran Hospital in Des Moines tells of importing live fish by plane. All died during the long flight. So now they put a catfish in the tank. It prods them to keep moving. All arrive alive.

Advent
At a church meal after a funeral a man told me they were expecting a baby any time now, so each night in cold, cold Iowa, he removed the battery from his car and kept it in the house where it would be warm and ready to start the car. Might we anticipate the coming of the Christ-child with such eager and careful anticipation.

Alert
The Dow Chemical Company in Pittsburg, California, had a leak of chlorine gas when a gasket broke in a one-inch pipe. About 75 to 80 pounds of chlorine went into the air — not enough for a serious health risk. Yet the company and county took no chances and set off the emergency alert system. Sirens blew and a computer called all of us residents who live nearby with instructions to "shelter in place." It means to stay indoors, tape cracks, close windows and doors. In about three hours the "all clear" was sounded.

Hasn't the time come to sound the alert in our spiritual lives? Perhaps we ought "shelter in place" in our churches and then go out into the world to serve.

Angels
On an Air Wisconsin flight from Appleton, Wisconsin, I noticed they chain the tail down on a Dash 7 plane while parked. I suppose it is to keep the wind from moving it or lifting it up. We need prayerfully to consider what chains us down so we cannot or will not fly with God's angels.

Baptism
Former Bishop Blevins announced at the funeral of his 24-year-old son who had committed suicide: "Today we will claim Bob's baptism."

We do remain God's child regardless of our behavior.

*   *   *

On the road to Calmar, Iowa, a front yard had ice all over shrubs, grass, everything. This is April 19. Someone had left the lawn sprinkler on overnight and all had frozen into ice.

Could we scatter the water of Baptism like that? And let it plainly show and look beautiful?

*   *   *

When we moved from Des Moines to Berkeley, California, every single item had a tag fastened to it with its own number. It's Mayflower's system in case something gets lost along the way. There is a lot number and individual number for each item. As we moved into the President's mansion, every piece was checked off as received.

Would that we could be so diligent in tracking and keeping from losing every one of the baptized!

*   *   *

The Dean of the Church Divinity School of the Pacific and I came out of the common room and waited and waited for the rain to stop, only to discover the lawn sprinklers above us were on, causing it to appear like rain.

Perception and reality are often very different. Let's throw the water of baptism so broadly it appears as though it is a downpour.

*   *   *

I often watch in early morning as the doves perch on the upper rim of our fountain, waiting for the fountain to come on and the upper basin to fill so they can drink and bathe in it.

When it does finally come on, the upper basin must fill before any water flows to the larger lower one.

And so we do our ministry from the overflow of our Baptismal waters and many wait for us.

*   *   *

There is washing and there is washing. At a car wash today an elaborate sign described the prices for various wash jobs:
> Outside rinse only
> Outside double wash
> Outside with wax
> Outside with drying
> Outside and inside
> Add perfume to make it smell like a new car.

How much do we permit Baptism to wash us is also to be considered — outside only, inside with forgiveness toward others.

*　　*　　*

Joe Sittler on April 24, 1983, was asked how he would define Baptism. He said, "It is an enactment of the fact that you weren't consulted in the first place."

*　　*　　*

On *Real People*, two people who had been prisoners in the German concentration camp Dachau used the date of their release by the rainbow division of the U.S. Army as their birthday to celebrate each year. At the date of our baptism we were set free as well.

*　　*　　*

Gregg Davidson of Trinity Lutheran, Marshalltown, Iowa, came to our observance of the "Baptism of our Lord." We all made name tags which gave our name and date and place of our baptism. Gregg forgot to remove it and went next to Vets Auditorium for a basketball game. He said everyone was so friendly and even called him by name!

At our Baptism we are named and we join into a worldwide family of God.

Barrier

Our acolyte carrying the cross and leading the processional got to the chancel at Saint Johns and discovered the communion rail gate was still closed. Linda held the cross with one hand and opened the gate with the other. She then proceeded through but with the cross backward by then. How easy it is to erect barriers to the cross even in our church.

Bible

Palimpsest is parchment from which one or more writings have been erased to make room for late records. But erasers are not always complete so scholars reconstruct the dim fragments of letters partly erased and partly covered by subsequent texts. Reconstructing these records of the past and learning the stories which they contain is the task of those who write history.

There is a salvation history which is available to us thanks to those who were inspired to write it down as their own witness.

Blessings

There is a little steak house named Toppers in Des Moines, Iowa, between Mercy and Lutheran Hospitals. When I have my collar on, they always slip an extra piece of steak under the regular order (special). It's a real bonus just for being there.

What are the bonuses of our regular lives?

*   *   *

Some boys in a ski boat needed a tow. I went over and towed them into a nearby marina. They offered to pay. I told them just to purchase a tow rope and carry it in their boat.

We who have been forgiven from the cross ought to forgive others; we who have been so richly blessed ought to bless; we who are so loved, to love ... and so forth.

*   *   *

At the Batak celebration of pregnancy, birth, marriage, ordinations, or a very special visit called a Hula Hula, all sit on straw mats on the floor and eat with their fingers and drink. Speeches are made and when the speaker says something especially wise and worthwhile all assembled say in unison, *"Ima tutu,"* which means "May it be so!"

16

The Beatitudes in Matthew 5 are the *Ima tutus* of Jesus. Blessed are the poor, those who mourn, who grieve, and so forth. *Ima tutu.* May our ministries make it be so.

Boundaries
Merrill Lynch's ad on television: "We believe your world should know no boundaries." — 1987

... but we erect so many: economic, racial, nationality, left-over hatred, wrong perceptions, and so forth.

Brother And Sisterhood
During the Gulf War Peter Jennings told of an Iraqi family in Texas who named their first son Saddam Hussein and the second son born during the war George Bush. They told Jennings it was their prayer that they too one day should be brothers.

Burden
On an Ozark flight from Des Moines to Saint Louis in March, the plane had to be de-iced before we could take off. They sprayed alcohol on the plane from a highlift to knock off the snow and ice and lighten the plane for takeoff and for better maneuverability.

We have those things we need to remove from our lives which keep us from taking off and flying high as we are created to do.

Call
A young man working as church van driver, Larry Kennedy, locked himself out on the roof of Park Place in Des Moines, Iowa. He called for help and they couldn't locate the source of calling. Men on the parking lot said he deserved to be out there. Others waved and smiled. He was out there two hours before finally someone figured out his problem. We often misunderstand or fail to hear our neighbor's call for help. How many remain there alone and discouraged?

* * *

Kathy Gulbranson, a Pacific Lutheran Theological School student, was giving a children's sermon about the call. Holding up

17

a telephone, she asked the children, "... and how do we dial for Grandma and Grandpa?" The answer from a little one was, "... be sure to dial 0 first, so they have to pay for it."

*   *   *

In Steinbeck's *Grapes of Wrath* on PBS television, the preacher said, "I used to have these channels swarming with people baptized. I'm not a preacher anymore. I lost the calling. I used to have it, but I don't have it anymore."

The call is to be a disciple and we must be good stewards of the call itself.

*   *   *

In the musical, *Fiddler on the Roof*, Tevye says, "I know we are the chosen, but couldn't you once in a while choose someone else?"

John 11 answers that Jesus chooses us — but there is more than privilege in that choice. There is also real responsibility.

*   *   *

After the lacing of Tylenol Extra Strength with poison in Chicago, there began to be what the police called "copycat" crimes.

We ought to live out our call as copycats of the good ministry of others like Saint Francis, Joan of Arc, and Mother Teresa. And perhaps in the practice of our discipleship we might inspire others to "copy" us.

*   *   *

Tom Brokaw on the NBC evening news told of a Terry May on Thanksgiving who was at his brother's home for the big meal and had forgotten to turn on his beeper. Meanwhile the Tucson hospital had lungs and heart for a transplant for him. They put the message on the televised Dallas Cowboys football game. A neighbor saw it and came over and told him the hospital was looking for him. A helicopter was dispatched which took him to the hospital for a successful transplant. God shows the same kind of individual attention to us. The call comes over and over in many different ways.

Caring

On a recent airline trip I saw the Columbus control tower hold up the takeoff of our 727 stretch for a tiny two-seat Cessna 140 to land. About the same time an "expedite crew" brought one late bag out from the dock and loaded it on board a United 737 aircraft. Large is not always the factor in the kingdom. God expedites our salvation and cares for us like important people.

* * *

In an Advent retreat on preaching, the leader asked people to state what they would like Advent to bring them. One pastor startled the rest by calmly stating: "I would like to have my wife and lover back!" She had multiple personalities. It made the rest of the desires pale in comparison.

Centering

I tried to use my power skillsaw today. The round blade was just a fraction of an inch off center, so when the saw started, it vibrated and shook me and the lumber. I centered it and it ran like a top! It was smooth, and it cut great as well. Now what must I do to get back on center in my spiritual life? What is so off the center it vibrates others' lives as well?

Change

There is a town in Iowa named Correctionville. The surveyor has to make an adjustment every so often, because the earth is round. It needs to be about the width of a lot and half. State Route 32 follows this jog. Correctionville, Iowa's motto is: "Come jog down our street."

We need to make corrections in our straight lines and allow for adjustments in other lines also.

Character

The May 2, 1997, Antioch *Ledger Dispatch* told of an overturning in Oakland, California, "When an armored truck collided with a car and bags of money fell onto the street, delighted passersby seized on the windfall. The noon-time accident Thursday led to a mad dash for cash ... Women stuffed bills in their purses and motorists filled bags with dollars and coins." Geno Lucas said: "I heard a big crash. The truck was on its side. The door popped open and bags came out." Police said more than $100,000 was missing.

Some who took the money turned it in to their pastor. The television news that night claimed many were caught on the truck's security television cameras.

Our real test of character is often what we do when we think no one sees us. But God sees. And in many instances there are others who see our action as an example for them. God gives us strength and a sense of right when we think no one sees us.

The Christ

During the sermon at Saint John's Lutheran in Des Moines, Iowa, a homeless vagrant came through the chancel door and knelt before the altar and crossed himself. The ushers were confused as to what to do. I told them to let him alone — "He could be the Christ in our midst." After a few minutes he got up and left the same way he came. I can't remember the sermon contents, but I remember that dirty, disheveled man in our chancel that morning and wonder — could it really have been the Christ?

Christian Family

I like being a Christian because everywhere I travel I'm family at once. We are like the Visa card lines on television: "It's everywhere you want to be."

Christian Life

In the movie *Back to the Future* a young man goes back in time thirty years and sees his parents growing up. It becomes obvious that to know the future or the present does not enrich it. God has created us in time not to know the future so life now is more vital, interesting, and full of surprises.

Christmas

A favorite story at Saint John's, Des Moines, is about the Christmas Eve that Pastor Louis Valbracht wanted to let a doll down from the chancel ceiling and into a manger in front of the altar. He was preaching and gave the signal to Pastor Louis Piehl, who stood to the side with a fishing rod and reel to let the baby Jesus down. All went well until Piehl ran out of line about one foot short of the baby's being at rest in the manger. Finally Valbracht came out of the pulpit and pushed the doll into the manger, which pulled Piehl out into the chancel. He ran back to the wings, which pulled the baby back in the air, and so on! How many secular forces try to keep the baby from coming again this year?

* * *

Some years ago a submarine sank off the coast of Portsmouth, New Hampshire. When divers located it they heard a faint tapping from the inside. There were still some sailors alive inside the sub! In Morse code they communicated their crucial question: "Is there any hope?" The coming of the Christ at Christmas taps back: There is hope, for we have Emmanuel.

* * *

At the DeSoto wildlife preserve in Iowa I observed a highway employee driving a pickup truck along the side of the road and with a cloth polishing the reflectors on posts marking the side-ditch's edge. At Christmas we polish up again that light which came to us who live in darkness.

* * *

One Christmas the movie *Back to the Future* was being promoted and shown. We often celebrate Christmas in a backwards glance as what has been, without considering what this means for our, and the congregation's, future.

* * *

On NBC news, the director of the stage play *Annie* said, "I took a flat newspaper cartoon character named Annie and put flesh and blood on her." Martin Charnin was describing incarnation. The word became flesh. The word became flesh and blood in the person of Jesus.

*   *   *

On CBS news a man by the name of Al Copeland in New Orleans had millions of lights in his front yard for Christmas. One thinks first, how beautiful! Then it's reported the neighbors are suing him for disturbing the peace.

I think the light of Christ is like that. When we really let it shine, those who prefer the darkness will always complain and try to extinguish the light.

*   *   *

I took my son and wife and grandson to the airport today. It's the day after Christmas and the place was jammed. The birth of the Christ child still has the power to move people in great numbers all over the world!

Church

The church of the New Testament is no longer a territorial church but a church of all people, a church which has its children in all lands and gathers them from every nation. It is the one flock of the one shepherd, called out of many folds (John 10:16), the universal — the truly catholic — church which flows through all time and into which all people pour.

*   *   *

Danny only had one arm. He came to the second grade Sunday School class for the first time. When the teacher thoughtlessly asked the students to fold their hands and sing, "This is the church, this is the steeple," Hannah, next to him, saw his dilemma. Putting her fingers and hand in his, she remarked, "Come on, Danny, you and I will be the church together."

Oh, if we could only live it out as adults! Let's put our hands together and be the church.

*   *   *

On Riverside Drive in Des Moines, there is a board suspended over the street just nine feet high. A little farther on is a railroad bridge nine feet above the road. So the board checks your clearance before you get to the bridge. The scripture and the church give us a clearance test for our Christian journey.

* * *

I dictated my sermon "... like the disciples on the mount of Ascension." Cindy, the church secretary, typed it, "like the disciples on the mount of dissension, we will return to our ministry." We can turn Ascension's glory into dissension's misery.

* * *

It was explained to me today that the louvers in our parking garage ramps will automatically open up when the carbon monoxide level reaches a certain concentration. The ramp is then aired out of the dangerous gases. Perhaps the church ought to have something similar to ventilate the stale and dank air of a museum and bring in the fresh air of the Spirit.

* * *

On a PBS television episode titled "God and Politics: A Kingdom Divided," Joe Aldrich, a Methodist missionary in Honduras, said to Bill Moyers, "There is a profound relationship between our religion and our Sunday dinner."

It's easier to disconnect the inside of the church from the outside.

* * *

American Express advertises: "Membership has its privileges."

Can we claim the same for the church? Perhaps that which we think of as responsibilities are really privileges.

* * *

At a Memorial Day weekend speech at the Rotary Club of Des Moines, the General of the National Guard explained the use of the army rallying point. When troops go out to fight, if they get lost or scattered, the rallying point is a pre-arranged place like a fork in the road, high building, bend in river, and so forth, where they all meet again and rally before going back into battle.

23

Where are the rallying points of our battlefield lines? Which others meet us there to rally with us?

* * *

Today I saw a crew of men with air hammers tearing out the front steps and the approach to Debra Heights Methodist Church. There are those who work on behalf of the power which works against God to wreck the approach to the church. They hammer away with the power of the world. Sometimes it is on purpose. Other times it is without knowing what they are doing.

* * *

According to the Helena, Montana *The Independent Record*, the 1988 Pinocchio Award from the National Liars' Club Hall of Fame went to farm columnist Russ Hoy who said: "The 1988 drought was so bad that the Baptists were sprinkling and Presbyterians were using a damp cloth for baptism. The Lutherans were passing out rain checks and at least one Roman Catholic priest was trying to turn wine back into water! Authorities had banned water skiing in the Platte River because it was kicking up too much dust."

Our denominational differences must be as outlandish to God's Holy Spirit and those outside the church as well.

* * *

On United Airlines Flight 527, from Chicago to Oakland, we had to stop in Las Vegas to get more fuel. The high, strong jet stream we were bucking all the way across the country had used more fuel than usual.

We often need refueling because of bucking the forces that work against us. It's a good reason for regular worship and personal devotions. It's not wise to gamble running on empty.

* * *

Rev. James DeLange told at Sierra Pacific Synod the story of two office employees who for ten years kept turning off and on a fan in a ventilating shaft. They just couldn't agree. Then a remodeling project revealed the fan wasn't hooked up to the electricity all along. We may battle for years over things in the church and not be hooked up to the Christ as well.

*   *   *

There is a little white frame church on Martin Luther King, Jr., Boulevard in Oakland. There is a Better Homes and Gardens realty sign out front. It led me to muse how one would describe a church for sale:

     Abundance of forgiveness
     Precious fellowship
     Security in eternal life
     Assurance of companionship
     Help for difficult decisions
     Real presence of Jesus at meals
     Life-changing worship
     Will throw the building in free!
     Need not have good credit record or references
     No shirt, no shoes, still service

*   *   *

A man went berserk and started firing at motorists from his balcony near the seminary. Sawyer Hall on our campus was taken over by the Berkeley police. Out of there they operated on the emergency. All were dressed in black, with big guns, lots of radios, an ambulance, and a fire engine as they all gathered there with the SWAT team.

After all, perhaps our churches are the command post out of which we rescue on God's behalf. And no doubt we have a different way of helping both the victims and the perpetrator.

*   *   *

James Forbes, preaching at the installation of the President of Pacific School of Religion, said: "If there were no PSR, these times in our lives would call for us to invent one now."

So, too, the church of Jesus Christ.

25

*   *   *

In a promo for a television show, *Class of '96*, someone says: "Your true birthplace is the place where you find out who you are. Havenhurst — I have come home to the place of my birth." In my relationship with the Christ I have found out who I am and how I am. In the Christian church I have come home to the place of my birth.

*   *   *

At an ordination and installation service I noticed the new pastor responds to the questions, "I will and I ask God to help me." I wonder how the ordinary congregation expects God to do that helping? I think it's through the congregational members. But do they know that and are they ready to be used by God to do the helping?

*   *   *

In Naples, Florida, a man ran his car through the front doors of the Roman Catholic church and stopped just short of the baptismal font. The paper said he was "mad at God." What reasons might we be mad at God and what's the answer God gives? Consider Job!

*   *   *

An AT&T television ad features a display the company sponsored at Ellis Island in 1990. It shows immigrants bringing along with them from their home country a treasure. "Because staying connected is important to all of us."

Belonging to God's family, remaining God's children, keeps us connected. We also have treasure which represents us and our heritage.

*   *   *

Billy Graham said it in his crusade in Alberta, Canada. When you are going to certain countries you must have a vaccination for cholera. The next day you get a little sick and a little cholera, which keeps you from getting the real thing. Now we can have a "little religion" which keeps us from getting the real thing.

26

In the way we live out our church membership it's possible to give people just a little and never know the real thing.

* * *

Richard Fisher in his book *Speaking of Jesus* (Fortress Press, 1981, p. 117) writes, "I once knew a young woman who regularly every Friday night broke into the church to pray. Many times I offered her a key to the building, but, no, as far as she was concerned churches were for breaking into. I never really understood the dynamics at work in her or in the congregation that caused her to see the church as a citadel to be stormed rather than a community to be joined." I wonder, also, how we are the church in our increasingly hostile culture.

* * *

Marvin Kalb on an NBC television special describing the shooting of the Pope said, "The Pope is most happy on Wednesday afternoon when he is with the people. They are his hallelujah people, his emotional flood." We clergy all need our hallelujah people as well. Congregations can do that for us.

* * *

I took Pastor Moses from Tanzania, Africa, to a Burger King restaurant. He asked the young employee there, "Are you a Christian?" She replied, "Oh, no, I'm a Baptist!" I wonder if our denominationalism may not get in the way of our Christianity at times.

* * *

I removed the strainer on our bathroom faucet, cleaned out the tiny pieces of gravel, and replaced it. We now got three times the flow and pressure. Over a long period of time impurities had gathered in there, strained out of the water. The flow had reduced gradually over this time without anyone noticing. Now there is great flow again. I wonder what impediments have gradually reduced the flow of baptismal water of our churches and ministries?

                    *   *   *

Did you hear about the man who bought a stationary exercise bike and hired the neighbor boy to come in and ride it for him? Or the man who joined the church but never attended. He just mailed in his offering each month?

                    *   *   *

Pastor Brady Faggart told the Iowa Synod Assembly: "The church doesn't just preach the gospel, it is the gospel. We gather to be the gospel." So it is for the church to be defined as the body of Christ alive *in* and *for* the world.

                    *   *   *

Some jet engines on airlines have metal umbrellas on the back which the pilot can use like brakes. It changes the forward thrust to a reverse thrust with the same blast of air. God's *ruach* (or spirit wind) can be reversed to ugliness and hatefulness and dissension in a congregation as well.

                    *   *   *

The photographer for the 3:30 wedding arrived about 2 p.m. and saw the bride and groom greeting the guests after their 1 p.m. service. The photographer, thinking he was late, began to madly take pictures only to be told finally this wasn't the wedding for which he had been hired.

Comfort

Our maintenance man at the seminary fastened the large organ to the wall of the chapel with strong angle iron rods. It's in case of earthquake. We will play a tune that comforts us when the earth shakes beneath our feet.

Commitment

At the Kennedy Space Control Center there are signs which come on telling of the many countdown checks. Then at about fifteen seconds before lift-off the sign reads: "Commit." So too, in landing a plane, there is a time when it's too late to abort the landing and the pilot "commits."

Perhaps there are times like confirmation (affirmation of Baptism) when we are to commit with the help of the Holy Spirit.

Communion

I stood in the aisle of Saint Peter Church, Monrovia, Liberia, and inquired as to the fate of my former students and pastors observing the horrible bloody civil and tribal war. We were there to consecrate the new Bishop Sumoward Harris. Finally the old Pastor Bypu said of my inquiries: "Some have starved, others beheaded, others died of fright. But today when we gather for the bread and wine, they will all be here." And later on they were. Now that is the communion of Saints.

*   *   *

Kellogg's Corn Flakes now advises on their television ads: "Kellogg's Corn Flakes, taste them again for the first time."

Taking the bread and wine each time can be like that. Let's not lose the newness of it.

*   *   *

At Afton Alps ski area, approximately fifty feet from the end of the chair lift is the sign "Prepare to unload," and then at the end, "Unload here." We could erect such signs in the aisles of our church sanctuaries. And at the communion rail "Unload here," for all our sins may be dumped there. In worship we unload in preparation for starting over.

*   *   *

The movie *Places in the Heart* is the story of a southern woman trying to survive with her family after her husband is shot. It opens with the gospel hymn "This is my story ..." and closes with "In the garden" as they all gather for communion in church. You see the murderer, the Ku Klux Klan, an adulterer, a black and white couple all there for the bread and wine.

29

* * *

Boston Market currently advertises its food like the "Boston Carver" and ends the television ad with a woman saying, "Don't mess with dinner." What could we Christians say should not be messed with? Don't mess with Sunday. Don't mess with the sacraments. Don't mess with the Word. Don't mess with the table of the Lord where we commune with our God in the bread and wine.

* * *

While worshiping at Saint John's Lutheran Church in Antioch, California, I watched a little boy go forward for communion. He took the wafer and individual cup, and instead of eating and drinking there, he returned to his seat and held a little picnic back there. How might we take the true presence from our church's altar out into the world where we live, work, and play?

Communion Of Saints

Pastor Carlos Schneider tells of Ted and Tom, who sat in the balcony at Saint John's, Sacramento. Ted has died. Tom sits in the same place and keeps a place open for his deceased brother even when the balcony is crowded.

... "the communion of the Saints" lived out by Tom of Saint John's, Sacramento.

Companioship

60 Minutes on October 3,1982, had a piece on a recent study on the effect of having a pet. It showed that having a pet reduces blood pressure and that people even live longer. They are using them at Lima State Hospital to reduce the inmates' depression. People who live with someone else live longer, and are less subject to heart attacks.

Isn't there a ministry here? We disciples need companionship. We have it in the "Communion of Saints."

* * *

30

At the Johnstown, Pennsylvania, Holiday Inn restaurant I noticed an old homeless man looking in the window watching the well-dressed people eating their elegant and plentiful dinner. Perhaps we inside the church, all dressed up, look like that to those on the outside looking in.

Compassion

An ad for Pioneer in *Newsweek* shows a man and a woman in pajamas reclining on a couch reading the newspaper. The caption is: "We bring the revolution home." Under the picture are the words: "Sunday morning. Time to kick back, get comfortable and perfect the art of doing nothing. Ideal compassion. Pioneer's new six-disc CD player." We know a different peace and compassion.

* * *

The big fire at Thousand Oaks, California, was started by a homeless man trying to keep warm. Many million dollar homes burned to the ground. Perhaps they failed to take in the man.

We pay a price whenever we ignore the poor and homeless. Eventually it comes back to our own lives and homes.

* * *

On the CBS evening news, concerning the helping of Vietnam refugees, the newscaster said, "Americans are suffering from 'compassion fatigue.' "

Probably those who passed by the man in the ditch along the Jericho road were also. Dare we?

Conscience

We installed an alarm system in the faculty annex this week. If you don't punch in the code, and try to open the door or window, the siren on the roof sounds.

I notice so many have alarms in their cars now that when they frequently sound, no one pays any attention.

We need to build alarm systems in our own lives so they sound and we pay attention when our natural selves begin to drag us into unsafe places and actions.

31

Consider what silences our alarm or what sensitizes us to hear and take action.

* * *

At the Holiday Inn at the Columbus, Ohio, airport, a fire alarm went off in the night. Various reactions:

Some came out in night clothes right away. Some got dressed completely, then came out. Two pastors from Minnesota never did come out. They didn't know there was an alarm.

Some knew and just ignored it.

The fire department arrived in no hurry but had all the equipment just in case.

One couple with two children had just had a brother-in-law burn up in a motel fire. They came out with sheets wrapped around them.

There are alarms that sound in our lives and families and congregations; we respond differently.

Conversion

My medical doctor friend explained today how in medical terms the doctor must convert the heart when there is heart trouble.

We Christians have paid far too little attention to the need for conversion of our hearts. People join our churches like joining the local service clubs or with even less need to change the heart. Perhaps renewal and conversion need be recaptured as part of our spiritual lives.

Courage

Barbara Lundblad at an ELCA Assembly said: "The reason they tie mountain climbers together is to keep the sane ones from going home."

It is in family and the church we are together. We give one another courage.

* * *

John Wayne, born in Winterset, Iowa: "Courage is being scared to death and saddling up anyway."

Perhaps this kind of bravado helps if one believes it deeply enough.

* * *

On NBC news, Tom Brokaw told of a man in East Germany who said, when asked why he liked Mikhail Gorbachev, "Because for the first time in my life, I am not afraid." Our Emmanuel promised, "Be not afraid, I am with you always to the end of the age!"

* * *

A ballplayer for the Pittsburgh Pirates said he was not afraid. His parents had taught him: "No matter what, God still loves me. My parents still love me also." To be assured of being loved is one of the greatest gifts life can give us. It is one of the most profound shaping forces in any person's life.

* * *

A special program about Pope John Paul II tells about an assistant to John Paul when he was a bishop and the communists demanded work stop on a church at Mora Huta. The Communists said it could not be built. His assistant said he was afraid. John Paul replied, "Nicolei, fear only poor work." Sometimes our best contribution in the circumstances is to do our work well.

Cross

With the neighbor's financial help, we were able to cut down two huge eucalyptus trees which had died and stood near the seminary chapel. The surprise was that now the cross could be seen from way down the hill. I wonder what other things and schemes need be cleared away to let the cross shine in our own lives.

* * *

I noticed with Peter, our security person and student, an owl which perches on the cross of the chapel at night and hoots at us all. It's really different to see it there when the timer turns the floodlight on the cross. Who gives a hoot from the cross? The old owl does.

The Bible often speaks of owls: Leviticus 11:17; Isaiah 34:15; Psalm 102:6; Isaiah 34:11, 14.

*   *   *

A letter from missionaries and friends Barry and Alice Lang in Madan, Papua New Guinea, said, "Bilum is what people here use to carry all their personal possessions. The color and so forth indicate membership in a particular tribe. Mothers put their babies in them and hang them from a tree branch. The breeze rocks the infant to sleep. Jesus Christ carries his bilum of our heavy loads, mistakes, sins, worries, and problems. In many of our Lutheran churches a bilum is carved on the inside or outside as a constant reminder that Jesus carried our cross. We ought to help carry one another's burdens."

*   *   *

When we checked in at the Denver airport, I noticed the tag put on the luggage starts with the ultimate destination. It may get lost or even go a different route — but ultimately it ends up at the final destination. And how about us? Are we marked for the ultimate destination? Perhaps the sign of the cross at our baptism tags us too.

*   *   *

At a funeral of James Simmons I attended, Rev. Parish said, "I did not come today to preach a funeral — for we all preach our own funerals by the lives we live here. I came to share these few moments of tragedy with this family."

What a sobering idea that we prepare our own funeral sermons by the lives we live! But we also have a cross and Easter grace and a returned spirit to be with us now to get us through.

*   *   *

While on my way to a speaking engagement, I was worried about parish problems. The security machine at the airport went off because of my crucifix in my suit coat pocket.

There's the answer. We serve the Christ and it is him who sets the direction and our mission.

*   *   *

In the movie *The Thorn Birds*, after telling the story of the thorn bird, the priest said to Maggie: "... for the best is only bought at the cost of great pain." Jesus bought our at-one-with God at great pain on the cross.

Danger
At a very busy intersection today someone had hit the barricades where road work was being done. Cars were going down the street and hitting the hole in the pavement about eight inches deep with a tremendous thud. Someone had removed the barricades to a danger. Our culture continually removes barricades and each generation seems to have to locate the pitfalls for itself.

Destruction
A market sign over a shopping mall all boarded up: "This construction killed us." A new four-lane highway is now there. What we call construction, another might view as destruction.

Devil
I preached in Wozi, Liberia, one night through an interpreter into the Loma language. Wozi is in the center of animism. They had laid a vine around the entire village to keep me out. During my preaching the "Lion" came to town to try to scare my young listeners away from hearing the gospel. They also played drums and danced outside the building to drown out the gospel proclamation. But through all the fear and superstition we were heard, and the Holy Spirit moved some to believe. What noise competes with the gospel where you live and worship?

Discipleship
Mother Teresa of India said, "Unless life is lived for others, it is not worthwhile." That is the call of Jesus to live as his disciples and give our lives away for others.

* * *

In interviewing Hong Kong Christians about how they were preparing for the Chinese takeover in July 1997, I heard some inspirational answers. Their solution is to learn all the Bible they can in case they don't have access any longer, to learn how to minister to each other in case there are no pastors, and to learn how to witness to the gospel so that the faith might live on. Oh, that we in the United States might sense that same urgency in the practice of our faith.

*　　*　　*

I saw an ad for a brake and muffler shop that read: "We stand behind our exhaust systems and in front of our brake systems." Just like that, people must read our lives of discipleship as having integrity. The Native American calls it "walking the walk and talking the talk."

*　　*　　*

There is a commercial for Honda lawnmowers which tells of a test each of their mowers meet: "the Clara Johnson test." It must start on the first pull by Clara. What test do we insist on in our lives? The Christian lifestyle, the discipleship test, the "if Jesus were watching test"?

*　　*　　*

My friend Joel Teigland showed me a copy of a letter of recommendation written by a professor of medicine in South Carolina which stated, "His value system rests soundly on his Christian beliefs which are secure, not requiring any public show." A good description of the Christian disciple.

*　　*　　*

Larry Mize on April 12, 1987, won the Masters golf tournament at Augusta, Georgia, in a sudden-death playoff with Greg Norman. The chip shot bounced a few times and the crowd began to cheer long before the ball went into the cup — a 140-foot shot! It was a lot like hitting a home run or bowling a strike and somehow knowing it before it is completed.

Is this possible in answering the call to discipleship? Can we feel the spirit's assurance early? Or God's will?

*   *   *

The Chaplain at PLTS, Ben Borson, once told of a man who hated his wife's cat so much that he took it out and drowned it. To soothe his wife's feelings he offered a reward for the "lost" cat. Those who knew he didn't like the cat ridiculed him for offering such a large reward. He replied, "If you know what you know you can take some risk."

Knowing of crucifixion and resurrection we can risk a venturesome discipleship.

*   *   *

Today are more hearings for U.S. Supreme Court Justice nominee Clarence Thomas. I wonder what a hearing for a Christian would be like who was nominated to be a disciple.

*   *   *

PLTS Chaplain Ben Borson said: "When you invite Jesus into your hearts he does not come in alone." Put that with Marriott Hotel's claim "Service, the ultimate luxury," and you have the life of a disciple.

*   *   *

Our granddaughter, Hannah Marie, came for a visit. When I got into the hot tub after her and commented, "Ouch, Hannah, this is really hot," she replied, "It's all right, Grandpa, it gets used to you." Perhaps we try to adjust too much to the world rather than live out our discipleship and let the world adjust to us (or not).

*   *   *

The Marines had an ad on television during the San Francisco 49ers and the New Orleans Saints football game: "The few, the proud, the Marines." What might be an ad for disciples of Christ: "The few, the humble, those who serve, Christ's Disciples."

*   *   *

On the freeways of California they speak of the "rubber neck effect." It means the slowdown of traffic because of drivers gawking at an accident or a car pulled over by the state patrol.

Could we live out our discipleship in a way which would slow down the world as they observed our priorities and deeds?

I wonder if there was a rubber neck effect when the Good Samaritan helped the man in the roadside ditch?

*   *   *

In a D-day special over CBS, Dan Rather was talking with Norman Schwarzkopf. He told how the paratroopers were dropped at night and given little metal crickets to use in identifying each other in the dark to find out if a troop were friend or enemy.

What can we offer to identify our discipleship and allegiance?

*   *   *

We had three beautiful oak trees in our backyard. But when the house was built the contractor put fill dirt around them and ran a heavy bulldozer over the ground over them. They began to die. We had to trim out the dead wood, drill holes toward the roots, insert fertilizers, and dig out the fill dirt around them to allow them to breathe. God furnished the rain that summer — beautiful leaves and health returned.

Christian education calls for the same drastic action with the roots of our members. Disciples need be fed and trimmed and nurtured like those trees. And some have had their lives packed down hard from being run over and over.

*   *   *

I noticed at Chicago's O'Hare Field the pilot has two neon lights, orange and red, to line up. When the pilot does that the plane is parked in exactly the right place. I believe it's that way for discipleship. Get stewardship and evangelism in the right proportions in our lifestyles and we are at the right place.

*   *   *

There is a light on each table at Bishop's Cafeteria in Des Moines. A sign says "For further service push button." When the waiters see the light on, they come to help. Would that we could see the lights burning for those in our community who need service. It's a light calling for our practice of discipleship.

*   *   *

A motto right now for John Deere lawn tractors is "Some settle for second best." Then compared are:

    rowboat and yacht;

    hose and tub and a swimming pool;

    tiny camera and one with a telephoto lens;

    then a little power mower compared with a John Deere.

Wow! The second best in our discipleship often crowds out the possibility of the very best.

*   *   *

A child named Amy was asked in Sunday school what she was doing. She replied she was "... drawing a picture of God." Her teacher told her she couldn't do that; no one knew what God looked like. She replied: "They will when I get done." Perhaps the way we live out our discipleship helps paint a picture of God for those who see us.

*   *   *

I noticed on a cold winter day that the Life Flight helicopter has a heating blanket around its engine to keep it warm and ready to fly at any moment the call comes to do so. We need to keep warm our motivation to serve others no matter how cold our own lives may be.

*   *   *

When a knight came to the court of King Arthur, he did not come to spend the rest of his days in knightly feasting and celebration. He came reporting for duty, asking what mission he might be sent on which would be done for Arthur. So too our discipleship.

*   *   *

Joel and I were out to "bless the fields" with a little pheasant hunting. We came to an electric fence. Joel commented that it wasn't

39

hot. But I insisted he go across first. Throwing one leg over the fence, he came astraddle it, and he discovered it was "hot." So he jumped first on one leg then the other trying to get over or back. It's painful to straddle the fence and yet we often encourage it with a halfhearted following of the Christ and living in the world.

Diversity

The Indonesian national motto is "*Binneka Tuggal Ika*," which means "Unity in Diversity." This is for a country which is 86 percent Muslim! Is there not a unity of diversity in our practice of discipleship? And do we not derive a richness for our discipleships, including all sorts and kinds and colors of people? And isn't that what God intended all along for us Christians? The more diverse our fellowship, the more united God's spirit makes us.

Easter

There is a small church called Saint Peter in the Parish of Saint Andrew about one half hour from Kingston, Jamaica, near Fort Charles where the tombstone of one Lewis Gadly reads as follows:

"Here lies the body of Lewis Gadly who departed this life in Port Royal the 22nd of December, 1739, aged 80. He was born in Montpelier in France, but left that country for his religion and came to settle in this island where he was swallowed up by the great earthquake in this year 1692. By the providence of God was he by another shock thrown into the sea and miraculously saved until a boat took him up. He lived many years after in great reputation. Beloved by all that knew him and much lamented at his death."

We also have a new life in Christ available to us.

*   *   *

Five grown children kept the remains of their mother in her bedroom more that eighteen months after she died, filling the room with presents and flowers in the belief that she would be resurrected. Blanche Riley, 56, died in March 1990 in a second floor bedroom. A niece of Mrs. Riley in Florida grew suspicious about a family's claim that she was unavailable and had been sleeping a lot. Family members cleaned the remains daily, changing the bedclothes and

disinfecting the room to mask the odor. — *Oakland Tribune*
September 22, 1991.

Easter people have a better hope!

* * *

A television ad for Burlington Coat Factory: "Easter is almost
here. We have clothes for boys and girls" — a commercialization
of our celebration of resurrection.

* * *

There is a story told of a White House employee calling
Woodrow Wilson in the middle of the night and saying that an IRS
employee had died and asking if he could take his place. Wilson
said, "It's all right with me if it's okay with the undertaker."

Jesus took our place on Good Friday and Easter through
resurrection.

* * *

On CBS news with Connie Chung, she called it the Lenin
problem: "What to do with a God who failed." They have Lenin on
display. I saw him. Now what do you do with him? Bury ...
traditionalists say no. Our God is one who won in the Easter victory.
Not on display in a glass tomb, embalmed and preserved. No need
to display a dead preserved body. Ours is alive through us and the
church. We are the Easter People.

* * *

For my class in advanced preaching, Roger and I wheeled a
casket by a seminary classroom and into the chapel. It caused quite
a stir in the class. Perhaps eschatology needs more emphasis in all
our theological studies. The casket brought the discussion very close
to the ground! It was for my students to use in preaching a practice
funeral sermon.

It's especially true that the awareness of life's brevity brings
an awareness of life's gift nature.

41

*   *   *

In a television movie titled *A Time to Live,* the son was dying of muscular dystrophy. When he knew he was dying, he asked to be placed in an impudent position. They sat him up in bed and he died. "Impudent" is sometimes defined as presumptuously confident and self-assured.

We face death like that also because we anticipate Easter and our resurrection.

Emmanuel

On an episode of the formerly popular television sitcom *Night Court*, Mac, the black court bailiff, said to a woman covering for her husband's suicide by confessing to murder: "Beyond a man's limit is a place where God doesn't want us to be alone."

So God's Emmanuel and the Holy Spirit with us.

*   *   *

A mother brought her son to a concert to hear a great pianist. At intermission the little boy broke away, went up on stage, and began to play "Chopsticks" on the grand piano. A spotlight was placed on the little lad and the crowd got quiet. The boy became very afraid. The maestro saw it from the wings of the stage, came out and sat on the bench with the boy, and began to play the upper part of "Chopsticks." He leaned over and whispered, "It's all right now, son. I'm with you."

God comes and sits with us and sees us through.

*   *   *

Heard at a Wittenberg University board of directors' meeting: There was an ice skating contest. One skater fell and slid across the ice and into the row of judges, upsetting them. After getting themselves together, they all gave her zeroes except one who gave her a nine! When asked why the nine, the judge replied, "You must remember it's slippery as hell out there!"

It is slippery out there, but we don't have to skate alone.

*   *   *

42

1988 — Dan Jansen, skating since the age of four, fell twice in the winter Olympics. His sister had just died of leukemia. In his hometown, people at the local bar said: "When he fell, everyone fell with him." His dad said, "Our heart was in our throat." At the bar the townspeople were cheering him, "Come on, Danny!" — Mark Phillips on the CBS evening news.

God's angels cheer us on. The fellowship has their Christian hearts in their throats. We do not go out there alone.

*   *   *

On the television program *60 Minutes*: Laurence Olivier at the age of 59 still got stage fright and always had someone stand in a certain place in the wings so he could see the person. He told him, "If you are not there, I shall run."

We have the Christ and his people always standing in the wings for us. We never need run.

*   *   *

While sleeping in the guest house of the Lutheran Church of Liberia in Monrovia, I would hear a clinking sound outside my window. When I asked about it, I was told the night watchman taps his machete on the fence every so often to let rogues and bandits know he is there and also to signal those inside that they are safe in the scary dark of night. God taps out this message for us. We are okay. Emmanuel is with us.

Envy
In *Newsweek*: "Executive Robert McDonald, after cleaning up after his dog, took literally a mugger's demand to 'give me what you got.'

"He must be New York's dumbest mugger!" (*Newsweek*, November 9, 1987, p. 21).

We almost always overvalue what the other person has.

Ethics

There is an unwritten code of the Bataks of Sumatra that dictates right and wrong behavior. It's called the *adat*. It governs their ethics, morals, and social protocol. It is a very strong force in the life of all Batak Christians as well. Often the *bius* will interpret just what the *adat* is in a particular situation and will mete out the proper punishment if the rules are not obeyed. The young often learn the *adat* not by reading it in a book, but rather, seeing it practiced by others who follow it.

We Christians have an *adat* also. It is learned by how we live out our lives of discipleship consistent with Christ's interpretation of God's commands. We must always ask how well we are passing on our *adat* to the next generation and to new Christians of any age.

Evangelism

I was at First Methodist Church in Des Moines for a meeting. In a cupboard off the church parlor was a sugar bowl with a note taped to it: "Evangelism sugar."

What is the sweetness we bring with the gospel?

Pass the sugar, please.

Example

I saw a man today pushing his four-year-old son across the street at Forest and Harding against the light.

What is that child learning from his father?

*   *   *

In a little town in Missouri they spread oil mixed with dioxin, a toxic impurity in herbicide, on the dirt roads. It was to prevent dust. Now the Environmental Protection Agency is buying the whole town to protect the people from the effects of dioxin.

What we spread can be healing or toxic, but we rarely buy it back to protect those we love.

*   *   *

44

A little Asian girl twiddling her thumbs was observed at the Washington, D.C., airport. She was sitting next to her father and mimicking her father, twiddling her thumbs at the same speed as he. He would slow up; she would slow up. He would move them rapidly and so would she. He never noticed.

Little people watch us and often copy our actions. It's a big responsibility to be an adult whom children watch.

Faith

In southern Egypt the temples are built on the east side of the Nile where the sun comes up. On the west side of the Nile where the sun sets are the tombs. Where are we building our faith temples?

*   *   *

A representative of the WCC USA said to the ELCA constituting convention in Columbus, Ohio, that he was brought up on the Heidelberg Catechism, so: "On good days I read Calvin and on bad days I read Luther."

*   *   *

The Philistines thought Goliath was so big he could not be defeated. David thought him so big he could not miss him.

David's faith was the difference.

*   *   *

"Sometimes you have to leap and build wings on the way down." I heard it said in a restaurant in Mesa, Arizona. But it ought be whispered daily to us who are timid in faith.

Faith And Action

At a PLTS chapel service Christine Sinnott talked of an eagle stirring up its nest. She went outside and saw four eagles soaring over Tilden Park Hills in an updraft. What if when we walked outside church we always saw it happening?

*   *   *

"When we don't speak for ourselves, someone else will speak for us," said Jill June of Planned Parenthood of Iowa. She added, "When we don't act, others will act for us." Perhaps this is what church mothers and fathers meant by sins of omission.

*   *   *

Dan Rather told of the rising water in Salt Lake, twelve feet higher in the year of 1987. Christians got together and prayed. Engineers built a viaduct and pumped it out to another lake in the desert! There is a time to pray and a time to be the instrument through which God answers prayers. Get up off your knees and get busy!

*   *   *

I recognized a police officer, Gary Cowger, of Des Moines, who saved a little boy by diving in and pulling him out of a lake. A police officer who was a member of the congregation, Dan Dusenbery, was asked to read the scripture. He was very frightened to do so but did because I asked him. After the service at the door I overheard Dan telling Gary, "The next time, you read the Bible and I'll jump in the lake."

There are times which call for reading the word and there are times just to jump in.

*   *   *

We relocated the thermostat from the drafty hall to the living room today. There is a big difference between a thermostat and a thermometer. One feels the temperature and takes the necessary action to change it. The other just tells you the temperature but does nothing about it. It's the difference in the way we often respond as well. Complain and do nothing or offer to help make the necessary improvement.

*   *   *

Professor Robert Smith told of his family's being at a wedding. While the homily was being preached, a little granddaughter fed all the family in her pew Cheerios® and had them join hands during the prayer. The preacher was talking about it and this little girl was doing it. Feeding and bringing together, ministry indeed!

*　*　*

On *60 Minutes*, March 14, 1982, Theodore Hesburgh, President of Notre Dame University, quoting Dante said, "The worst place in Hell is reserved for those who remain neutral during a moral crisis."

Saint John talks about neither hot nor cold which he spit out.

*　*　*

In an NBC special on *The Life of Florence Nightingale*, there was a war between Russia and England in 1853. Nightingale felt "called by God" to go to Turkey to help care for the soldiers as a nurse. "You will be going to a country in the worst of circumstances." Florence replied, "No, the worst of circumstances would be to do nothing." It's still the worst of circumstances for Christians to do nothing.

Richard Mills, whom she loved, wrote to her as she was about to leave: "Florence, hold your head high — few of us can ever say, 'I made a difference' — you are one of those few."

Faith And Life

Dr. Hellman, a psychiatrist on a television show titled *Relentless Mind of a Murderer*, said this: "Life is the process of finding out too late what should have been obvious at the time."

But the life of faith can help it come out differently.

Family

On a television sitcom, Mrs. Ann Romano said after a tough day with the children: "All of this for a Whitman Sampler on Mother's Day." — *One Day at a Time*.

To be a parent and Christlike is not easy but worth much more than an annual box of candy.

Forgiveness

After consecrating the elements at Saint John's one day, I made my way toward the balcony with the elements to administer

47

communion there. A member who did not like me and always tried to avoid taking communion from me was coming down the steps. He came around the corner and we collided.

I spilled the intinction wine on him and myself. It's one of the reasons we have the sacrament: the blood was shed not only for God's forgiveness of us but for our forgiveness of each other. However, we never did reconcile our differences.

* * *

I was very moved today to see on the news Reginald Denny hug the mothers of the two boys who had beaten him nearly to death during the Los Angeles riots.

We rarely live out our conviction that, because God radically forgave and loved us, we are to do the same toward each other.

* * *

From *On Golden Pond*: Ethel says to her daughter about her old father, Norman: "Sometimes you just have to look at a person and remember he is doing the best he can."

What good advice about how imperfect sinners ought to see other imperfect sinners.

* * *

In front of Boswell's restaurant on Harding Road in Des Moines at 8 a.m. there was a blue Volkswagen Rabbit parked next to the street. In the rear window was a sign: "I was wrong." Inside the window: "I am sorry."

For us forgiven sinners, it is often necessary to admit we were wrong and we are sorry. I wonder if in this case it was said in time?

* * *

Barbara Walters of *20/20* interviewed Mr. and Mrs. John Hinckley, Sr., parents of John Hinckley, Jr., who shot Press Secretary James Brady, two secret service agents, and President Ronald Reagan.

When asked if they had any words to James Brady and the secret service agents shot in the assassination attempt, his parents replied, "Yes, we are very sorry." Then asked if they had any words to their son who shot them, "Yes, we love him very much."

Love the sinner; hate *only* the sin.

*   *   *

The news tonight was very moving. It pictured the families of the boys who beat a baby nearly to death and the parents of the baby, brought together by a black pastor. They hugged, cried, and prayed together. One family was African-American, the other Mexican-American. There is a way for all to be one family in Christ and to give forgiveness even to those who most hurt you.

*   *   *

Missionary Barry Lang at Bong Mine, Liberia, tells that when a Liberian Christian lives the wrong way or when two people have a difference of opinion and have strong words, or one proves the other wrong, then he kneels on the floor and takes the foot of the other and begs for forgiveness. When the offended puts a hand on his shoulder, it is finished, "cut" — no more can either bring it up again. It is completely over! On the cross Jesus put his hand on our shoulder and proclaimed "it is finished" ... we are forgiven.

*   *   *

In a *60 Minutes* television segment, Archbishop Desmond Tutu of South Africa was being interviewed. They asked Tutu about how the Council of Reconciliation was being run by him. He explained that if those who committed atrocities during the time of apartheid would confess their sins, they would be granted amnesty from the council and the present government. The reporter asked, "Archbishop, isn't this carrying your Christianity too far?" That is Christianity — we carry radical forgiveness way too far. It's what Jesus taught us from the cross and after the resurrection. Carrying it that far makes us unique in our discipleship.

*   *   *

In the Batak language of Sumatra there is no word for surrender. It is also very difficult to say "I'm sorry" in Batak. But in the language of the cross we can surrender to the one who sacrificed his son in order that we might use the words often: "I'm sorry."

*　　*　　*

Staples, the office supply store, has a television ad which always ends with the slogan, "Yeah, we got that." What are people shopping so desperately for in their lives? Grace, forgiveness, peace, friendship, salvation ... "Yeah, we got that."

Foundation

I saw today a very heavy trailer of a tractor-trailer combination without the tractor parked on an asphalt parking lot. The front support wheels were sinking deeper and deeper into the asphalt and may have already gone all the way through. The driver of the trailer probably thought it a solid foundation on which to park the trailer — but not so. Check your foundation. "On Christ the solid rock I stand, all other ground is sinking sand."

*　　*　　*

While in Amsterdam, I noticed how crooked many of the houses (especially around canals) are. They are braced with large logs up the front of the building. God's presence can support us and we ought to support each other.

Freedom

Ralph Klein told the Senior Pastors Conference in Scottsdale, Arizona, that the custom of raising the hand as a pledge we are free came from the practice of raising arms to show there are no tattoos on the arms which would signal we are slaves. See Ezekiel 37:12.

In Christ there is a freedom.

*　　*　　*

Tegucigalpa, Honduras — "A Honduran peasant has been freed after spending nineteen years in prison because penal authorities did not learn that he had been acquitted in 1976." Gustro Adolf Amador, now 57, was charged in 1975 with stealing colored pencils from a marketplace in the capital, but a court acquitted him the following year. The written release order did not arrive at Tegucigalpa central penitentiary, where Amador was held, for the next eighteen years. — *San Francisco Examiner*, May 1, 1994.

Even though acquitted, we live as prisoners.

* * *

October 25, 1988 — The headline today is "Two Whales Break Free." The whole world's attention was on those whales that waited too long and were frozen in Alaska's icy waters. Americans tried dropping a weight from a helicopter to break a way to freedom. Eskimos who usually hunt them had cut breathing holes in the ice.

Finally a Russian icebreaker was used to crunch open a path for them.

One smaller and younger whale didn't make it. She just wore out.

The whales will still need to swim several thousand miles to get out of ice fields and danger before starting south to winter in Mexican waters.

Well, God focuses the same attention on us in our often deserved predicaments and wants to free us.

* * *

Our neighbor, architect David Frevert, always put his garbage bags on the trunk lid of his car and hauled them to the street on his way to work. One morning he forgot and proceeded downtown with two bags still on the trunk lid. I never asked when they fell or where, or what he did about it. We do carry with us a lot of un-needed garbage which ought to be dumped for our health and our well-being.

* * *

Pastor Helmut Hasse, who just retired as parish pastor after thirty years at the city church in Wittenberg, Germany, told of the day the Berlin Wall came down. During the worship service a man sat in the anteroom and listened to the radio. He came out and told Hasse the wall was coming down. The pastor announced the news of new freedom to the full church. He said they stamped their feet,

51

cried, hugged each other, and sang "Hallelujah." For a long time there was "no good order" in the sanctuary. Freedom at last.

* * *

The "time of changing" described to me by Pastor Helmut Hasse of the city church in Wittenberg all began as a little group there in Wittenberg, and even more so in Leipzig, gathering in the churches to pray for peace. There were so many, the Wittenberg police didn't know how to stop it. And the movement spread and eventually evolved into the fall of communism. It all began with a few of the courageous lighting candles in the sanctuaries of their churches.

* * *

In little Peace village in Sumatra they will show you a large haviara banyan tree where the "Apostle to the Bataks," Ingar Ludwig Nommensen, a missionary from the Rhenish Church in Germany, would buy slaves, give them freedom, and bring them into the Christian faith.

* * *

The *Datu* (medicine man) told the natives that the Goddess of Siatas Barita was angry with them and so they captured Nommensen and were going to kill him. A very strong wind and storm came up and he prayed and was freed. The one who purchased freedom for the poor was freed. God often frees those who are the instruments though which others are set free. Jesus bought our freedom on the tree of Calvary as well.

Friendship

"For the lonely man all the treasures of the world are no substitute for companionship. Narrower than a prison is the wide earth to an abandoned and lonely man ...

"Behold the Church! It is the very opposite of loneliness — blessed fellowship! There are millions of saints and believers who are blessed in it. No longer lonely, but filled, satisfied, yes blessed...."

—Wilhelm Loehe, *Three Books about the Church*
Translated by James L. Schlaf
Fortress Press, Philadelphia, © 1996

"Like candles, one after another in the bright circle of my friends goes out, the empty places turn dark, and seldom does another star fill the dark void." *Ibid.*, pp. 51, 52.

Future

The church sexton got the paper roll which plays the carillon bells in the church tower in the player upside down. It played continuously and a very strange melody indeed!

I think we often play a melody very strange to the rest of the world and one which goes backwards to shepherds, angels, camels, rather than forward to missiles, genetics, and nuclear challenges of the future.

Gandhi

Some memorable scenes from the great movie *Gandhi*:

He said: "Trouble is with eye for an eye, before long all the world is blind."

He said "Since we are all sinners, I'll leave the punishment to God."

He said "I'm in control with passive resistance. They are the ones out of control."

He walked to the sea to make salt, which was against the law. It was like Jesus riding the donkey into Jerusalem.

In South Africa as a young lawyer he was thrown off a train because he was colored.

When with high officials of the government, he took a tray from a servant and served them and the servant.

What a scene of his people walking up to the salt factory to be clubbed, and then the next line ... and the next ... and next.

He told a white Anglican priest, "Indians must do this; you can't do it for us."

There was the scene of Moslems and Hindus killing each other in India after independence. He said, "Religion seems to have caused so much bloodshed in the world."

Giftedness

On *60 Minutes* there was a special about "Savant Syndrome." People who seem mentally challenged in many ways have a brilliance about them: a man sculpts animals after seeing them once, a person plays the piano after hearing a piece once, a person has the whole calendar memorized. I met a young man in our Lutheran church in Phoenix who had all the cars' license plates in the parking lot memorized. The movie *Rain Man* tells of one of these. Is there not a special gift each one of God's creation has? And could not these special people have an extra measure of giftedness we ought to celebrate and benefit from?

*   *   *

In a television movie called *A Change of Seasons*, Pete said to his daughter: "We came alone, we leave alone. Everything else is a gift." I would like to add that the shortness of our lives here ought to add to our sense of the giftedness of life itself.

Gifts

Carolyn Rocco, daughter of the first president of our seminary, lost her stole at a restaurant and didn't realize it for a quite a while. The restaurant contacted to tell her. It was a gift. I wonder what gifts I have lost and didn't realize it.

*   *   *

I saw today missionary Jane Leidenfrost giving a cup of cold water at her door to several who came and asked for it. It was at her home of thirty years in Totota (ToToTa), Liberia. The words "cold water" are the name for a gift one gives to another after a service has been rendered. "... you have done unto me."

God's Love

While I was greeting people at the door as guest preacher for the day, a woman came up behind me, put her arms around my waist and hugged me, thinking I was her pastor, Ken Caudill. When she saw who I was, she simply recovered by stating that she always greeted her pastor with a hug, as it was often her only hug all week.

There are many lonely who come for companionship to God's house. They need to find a way to touch each other.

*　　*　　*

At PLTS, an East German organist named Sietzman said he lives in a socialist country and there people live alone. "Here people talk to each other and they even touch me. I feel good then and warm and together." After the PLTS community sang "A Mighty Fortress," he sat down and improvised "The Magnificat." Wow! Together our souls can magnify the Lord.

*　　*　　*

In the movie *Dead Man Walking* Sister Helen loved the condemned criminal regardless of his crime of rape and murder. She walked with him down the aisle to the chamber for injection to kill him. Others just couldn't understand a love like that. Wow! A powerful testimony to God's unconditional love for all sinners and how we must represent that radical love in our world and ministry.

*　　*　　*

My daughter Sarah lives in Washington, D.C. She agreed to meet me where the metros meet in the center city. It worked and we found each other. The old song goes: "Meet me in Saint Louis, Louis, meet me at the fair."

Where shall we meet as God's people? Where love and consideration for others intersect.

God's People

We walked five miles from ToToTa, Liberia, to a little bush village. The little mud church was too full and we had to move outside. Each person brought a lantern or flashlight, and several hundred sat on the ground to hear the gospel proclaimed under the starlit and moonlit night. They held a flashlight on my face and Pastor Manawu translated my sermon into Kpella. We were God's people and witness to God's word. Halfway around the world from home and church, but under the same stars and the same moon, we prayed and praised God.

55

God's Power

Not everyone enjoys Monday night football as much as I do. In 1997 the Green Bay Packers had an ad which shows a bunch of fans touring Lambeau Field. The guide runs his hand over the infield grass and says: "Feel the power," and the cheeseheads all smile.

We also have a power which the spirit wants us to have. That same spirit gives us the power to forgive, love the unlovely, get through grief, get over disappointment, have compassion for the unfortunate, and to love and love ... feel the power.

God's Presence

At a community Thanksgiving service at the First Methodist Church, Des Moines, the Drake University Choir sang the *Messiah*: "... he shall reign forever and ever ..." and left the sanctuary before the sermon.

The "forever" got shortened up a bit.

God's Word

"In every age the church with the Holy Scriptures at its side has had some witnesses to the truth and clarity of the Word of God who are more deserving of our trust than anyone who wears a cross and fine purple but contradicts the words of Scriptures." — Wilhelm Loehe

Good Friday

Retired Bishop Ronald Diggs of Liberia was arrested and told to stand trial on Good Friday. So all the Monrovia churches scheduled their Good Friday services for the court where he was to appear. On Thursday, they dropped the charges. The cross of Good Friday ought to free us — from sin, from guilt, from fear and shame.

Gospel

The Cathedral of Mexico City has a wire suspended from the ceiling to the floor with a plumb line weight on the end of it to show how far the building has moved and still is moving off center. I wonder if it could measure how much we move off the gospel center?

Grace

Because Dwaine Pittman was ill on the day we seven were examined before the confirmation, the questions Rev. Wessel had promised us were out of order. I gave the answers I had memorized anyway for each seventh question. Rev. Wessel never let on they were the wrong answers. What an example of grace he granted to us that day!

* * *

In 1719 the king offered what was called an "Act of Grace" to all pirates in the Caribbean. Calico Jack, one of the most notorious, took the offer. If they would give up their pirate's life, the king would give them amnesty and some land to settle on. It is an offer Jesus works on God's behalf from the cross.

* * *

A country song on radio has the line: "Somewhere between hell-raising and amazing grace." Perhaps that's a good description of where we humans live.

* * *

March 9, 1909, the city water tank in Des Moines collapsed and nearly washed away First Lutheran Church. After rebuilding, there was a foreclosure during the Depression and the congregation bought it back at a reduced price. It's now debt free. Our Baptismal water could have the power to move churches. Jesus has bought us back with a big price. We are debt free. All is forgiven.

* * *

I saw a Coptic priest, dressed all in traditional black, fall off a camel at the pyramids of Giza in Cairo, Egypt. Later I found out the camel's name was Grace. Even the best of clergy can fall from grace.

* * *

In an HBO movie *Tell Me What You Want*, Max Herschel's daughter tells him, as he tries to keep track of what his lover had done and was doing, "Don't keep books on people you love."

Like God's love for us, which is grace-filled, we accept the ones we love without demanding they live as we want. We accept them as they are.

*   *   *

I recall the first time I got a glimpse of the pyramids of Giza on the outskirts of Cairo, Egypt. I made the van driver stop so I could take a picture, but after a while as we got closer, I asked that he stop again for another shot. Several times we went through the same process as the three grand pyramids opened up before us. Grace is like that. It opens up wider and wider, grander and grander. Our first glimpse seems so small compared with now.

*   *   *

In a Christmas letter from a retired Denver pastor whose wife was seriously ill with cancer, the pastor quoted Frederick Buechner: "Listen to your life. See it as the fathomless mystery it is. In the boredom and pain of it — no less than in the excitement and gladness — touch, taste, smell your way to the holy and hidden heart of it because in the last analysis all moments are key moments, and life itself is grace."

Greed

At Drake University, Allen Boesak of South Africa said, "I'm here because some of us believe there is another America ... one which cares about our struggle."

Can we move above self-interest and greed?

Guidance

On a US Air flight from Johnstown to Pittsburgh on a small commuter plane, I noticed through the open door to the cockpit that both pilot and co-pilot put their hands on the throttle as they took off. God would put God's hand on ours as we fly together through dangerous and easy times.

Guilt

There is a scene in the movie *The Mission* in which Mendoza has killed his brother and Father Gabriel has dragged up the steep waterfalls a bag full of heavy metal armor. Finally at the top, the Jesuit missionary is freed by the cutting of the rope which was weighing him down. A beautiful picture of the heavy weight of sin and the freedom of believing in our Lord Jesus Christ.

Heart

On the outside of the Anthropological Museum in Mexico City are the words:

"God is as invincible as the night and as untouchable as the wind ... They were able/knew how to dialogue with their own heart."
—Aztec

Heaven

I watched them say good-bye for the last time. They were two old evangelists way up in the bush in Liberia, Africa, where I had transported Old Man Mopolu to see Mama "Ganna" (Amanda Gardner). She wagged her finger in his face and said, "Now, ol' man, don't you give up on this God business, and when we get to heaven all the people going to be there to greet us and give us a big hand clap." Might the same be said of all of us.

*   *   *

Tom Skinner at an Evangelical Outreach conference told us: "God's intention is that the church shall establish itself in an alien territory so people can see what heaven is like. We pray it in the Lord's Prayer. It's like when the English came to Africa and Africans could see what living in England is like." So each day let us live that others might glimpse into a vision of heaven.

*   *   *

Moses writes from Liberia about Old Man Mopolu, "He has the hope that he will one day meet you in heaven sharing with God your concern about him."

59

Help

In Tampa harbor one of the ships began to "list" badly. Three tugs were enlisted to push against the side in order to shift the water ballast. It was safe in the harbor but started to list and would have sunk.

It's probable when we feel safe in the harbor that we are most likely to be in worst damage. One tug could not have done it by itself but three together could and did.

*   *   *

On a portable air conditioner at the Oakland airport is stenciled the following: "If trouble light comes on, call the garage. Do not reset the air switch." So wouldn't it be good if we had a built-in trouble light which would come on ... and we'd seek help in resetting the course of our lives?

*   *   *

In the city of Nazareth I saw a young lad lose a load of clover tied on the back of a donkey. His father was scolding him severely for allowing it to happen, and in his anger struck him with a stick. I tried to help the boy reload the clover and he grinned appreciatively — but the father seemed all the more angry.

In that same town one matured who assured us that he would help make the load lighter. His father sent him to us not to punish but to help.

*   *   *

There are cables at the end of the runway of many airports to catch the plane out of control which could not stop in time. It's much like the turn-offs on the mountain roads of Oregon for truck drivers who have lost the use of their brakes. It's a long soft gravel lane with a large mound of gravel at the end to stop the truck.

We all need provisions and help to stop us when we run out of control. And to slow us down when we are running too, too fast.

*   *   *

We tried playing the sound of a crow in trouble to keep thousands of crows out of our trees around the church. It worked for a few weeks; then they came back and just ignored it. Steve Gunson explained how crows have strong tendencies to form habits like where they roost, and so forth. So they get used to about anything, even the cry of their own for help. And could it be of us as well?

History

According to the *Minnesota Star* newspaper, they train the Metro Transit Authority bus drivers by using a video of the route the driver will be driving. Oh, that the older Christians might serve as that video tape of the route the younger will transit.

*   *   *

On the Hertz bus at the Los Angeles airport there is a television in front that shows the driver what is behind the bus.

As we look at the past we launch ourselves into the future.

*   *   *

Dr. Kent Gilbert of the LCA told this story to pastor/evangelists. A wildcat strike was in progress against New York subways. People kept on going down the stairs to the subway, turning around at the bottom, and going back up. Those going up never told those going down it wasn't running.

This can be the way of history unless we tell our stories.

*   *   *

On NBC news there was a piece about restoring the Sistine Chapel in Rome. They built the scaffolding exactly as Michelangelo designed it. They have removed decades of grime and dirt and rediscovered vivid color.

The Christian life and faith can accumulate a build-up of years of habit, and so forth, which we must cut through so that the brightness might come through to us and through us to others.

Holy

There were two places in Amsterdam where there were big crowds but it was hushed: In the Van Gogh museum with all his

61

paintings, and in Anne Frank's home and hiding place. Where are the hushed places of our religious lives? What brings awe and reverence to us?

Holy Spirit

A televison commercial for John Hancock Insurance says: "We can help you here and now, not just here after."

The Christian can claim the same about the Holy Spirit. Not just for eternity, but equipment to live our lives to the fullest.

*   *   *

On a car at Methodist Hospital parking lot were two stickers: "Things go better with wine" and below: "Christians have more fun, especially later." Great to give out that kind of message about being a Christian; however, I would want to say about the second message: "Christians have more fun, especially right now." We often give the impression our faith is mostly for eternal life, while we have the Holy Spirit to equip us for life here and now.

*   *   *

Herbert W. Chilstrom, former Bishop of the Evangelical Lutheran Church in America, said: "Perhaps William Barclay is most helpful of all when he suggests 'paraclete' is derived from a term used by the Greeks to describe a very special person who went to war with the soldiers. He carried no weapons. His purpose was simply to be with the men as a source of wisdom, common sense, and encouragement. When the battle went badly, it was his task to remind them that only a battle had been lost and not the war. When they did well and came home heady with pride and overconfidence, it was his task to remind them they had only won a battle, not the war. In this role, 'the paraclete' was often the key to victory. His help at the right moment, his word of encouragement, his wise counsel were often the difference between victory and defeat." It is the role the Holy Spirit would play in our lives as well. (See John 15:26-27).

*   *   *

The strip of highly colorful and decorative cloth given as a special gift of friendship by the Bataks of Sumatra is called an *ulas*. At a wedding reception it is wrapped around the bride and groom as one. It is symbolic of deep, rich friendships kept warm in the future. Often woven into the cloth is "God's Peace." Like a blanket it is used to keep warm at night and to carry a baby slung over the shoulder in what is named a *parompa*.

We have a comfort of peace also and it's sometimes called the comforter, the Holy Spirit, which keeps us warm in spirit and peace-filled in struggle.

*   *   *

While conducting a discipling weekend at Richland, Washington, I noticed the use of the word "downwinder" in the local newspaper. Downwinder refers to the people who lived downwind of the nuclear reactors at Hanford during the 1940s when they were making plutonium. There are three counties where downwinders lived and are filing claims against the government for relief and health programs.

Do we have those who live downwind from our churches and ministries and whose lives are changed because of it? Or has the Holy Spirit's wind stirred at all in our communities because we are there?

Homeless

On December 28, 1984, National Public Radio reported that Jesse Carpenter was buried in Arlington National Cemetery with full military honors. He had frozen to death December 17 across the street from the White House at the feet of a friend who couldn't get into a shelter for the homeless.

How special to Jesus are the poor and homeless. We often overlook them right at our door.

Honor

In Andrew Lloyd Webber's musical *Evita*, which was made into a movie starring the infamous Madonna, there is a very moving scene near the end of her life. The masses loved Evita Peron and they wanted to honor her by making her vice president of Argentina. Knowing she was dying, she made a last appearance with her husband, Juan Peron, and said to the assembled adoring crowd at the palace Casa Roseda, "I must turn down your efforts to honor me and be content with having brought my people to the heart of Juan Peron." For us disciples it's the same: we must be content not with worldly honors, but with bringing our people to the heart of Jesus Christ.

Hope

Amy Grant, interviewed on CNN, was asked what the purpose of Christian music is. She responded that "... it is to lift people up."

Our preaching and witness to the gospel misrepresents the message if it does not "lift people up" and give them hope and promise.

* * *

Christopher Columbus tried to find a passage to India by sailing west from Spain. He got up the river which is now the Panama Canal as far as the *Santa Maria* would go and gave up and turned around. If he would have climbed the hill and looked over, he would have seen the Pacific Ocean, as Balboa did later. He missed the vision by so little. Defeated, he went to Cuba and then Jamaica, where two of his ships ran aground — approximately 1500 A.D. How often we give up too fast a little too soon.

* * *

"The theological paradox of our troubled time is that from the same traditions, beliefs, and practices now arise both the most heinous and the most humane attitudes and actions toward other individuals and groups. The task of the religious community is to distinguish the one from the other and to serve as a source of freedom, hope, and inclusion — to nurture the forces of life."
— Glenn R. Bucher of the Graduate Theological Union, Berkeley, California

* * *

Captain Gerald Coffer of the Air Force told how prisoners of war during the Vietnam war would tap out encouragement to each other by tapping on the cell plumbing. When the guy next to them was really hurting, they would tap out G.B. for "God Bless." G.B.A. meant "God Bless America." G.N. was "Good Night." Let us tap out good news to those in prison around us.

*   *   *

Linda Christensen called to say there was a beautiful rainbow in the western sky. It was a double one, aqua, yellow, and red. One end seemed on Saylorville Lake and the other at Saint John's Lutheran downtown. It was gone by 6:21 and then the rain arrived and God watered the good Iowa soil in the midst of God's promise of hope. Thanks, Linda, for pointing out and showing God's promise and beauty in our midst.

Humanity

At the formal academic ceremony of graduation at Wittenberg University, I saw a dog come behind the speaker's podium and drink out of the speaker's glass of water, then carry a cardboard box up the aisle. All of us seated on the dais wondered if the speaker would reach down for the glass and drink. He did not. But others see us quite differently than we sometimes suppose they see us.

*   *   *

Signs on three exactly same-looking doors at Augustana College, Sioux Falls, South Dakota:

Men-Women-Mechanical

Perhaps mechanical is close to being a third form of the human race. We must never lose our God-given humanness.

Humanness

On January 28, 1986, the space shuttle blew up one and a half minutes out of Cape Kennedy. That night on the NBC news: "Sometimes we aren't perfect and then there is a tragedy. And that brings us back to the fact again of our human frailty." President

65

Reagan said: "We don't hide or keep secret our space program — everything right up front. That's the price of freedom."

Human Worth

A letter arrived from Lydia Manawu in Liberia, marked, "No Monetary Value."

What is a person's worth?

Humility

Lee Kalmer, Dean of ISU College of Agriculture, told of a farmer buying a new tractor. He had it delivered at night so he could put on it the old decals so not to look new. He didn't want to "lord it over his neighbors." What an example of humble stewardship.

*　　*　　*

The author of *Ironweed* states: "It's a short distance from the 'Hallelujah' to the 'hoot.' " So it is we can come down fast and hard and painfully.

Humor

The Iowa State football coach told a story about a football game between centipedes and insects. The centipede was making all the plays in the second half. Coach asked, "Where were you the first half?" "I was getting my ankles wrapped."

*　　*　　*

Dr. Kent Gilbert told of turning off the freeway in Kissimmee, Florida. He pulled into a Burger King and asked at the counter, "How do you pronounce the name of this place? The boy said with great determination and very slowly: "B-u-r-g-e-r K-i-n-g."

Some things just aren't as complicated as they seem.

*　　*　　*

Oral Roberts, Robert Schuller, and Billy Graham all died at the same time and went to Heaven. There was not room for them for a few days, so they temporarily had to go to hell and wait until their place was ready. The Devil soon called and asked Saint Peter to get them out of there. Roberts had healed everyone, Graham had saved everyone, and Schuller had raised enough money to air condition the place!

Fun humor, but is it not so that our task as God's disciples is to do just that: to heal, to save, and to make conditions better for the less fortunate?

*   *   *

Jody Gast told me of God sending word to Moses that God sent the plagues as promised. "That's the good news. The bad news, Moses, is you will have to write the environmental impact report."

There is a need to consider always the impact of what we pray to God to take place.

*   *   *

Here is another funny sign. It is in a Midas muffler shop in Des Moines: "Please, let us know if you would like your old parts returned. Thank you. The shop manager."

*   *   *

The late Pastor David Ullery told me the story of two Salvation Army women who were at a convention and undressed to go swimming. "That's a strange navel you have," said one to the other. The other responded, "Okay, the next time you carry the flag."

We all carry a flag or flags for cause or causes in our lives. Often second best crowds out the very best for Jesus' disciples.

*   *   *

Al Haversat, a Lutheran clergyman, told of a man calling the florist and giving specific directions to prepare flowers for a casket with an extra wide ribbon, and so forth. When he got them he was astounded to find the directions on the ribbon, so it read: "Rest in peace on both sides and if there is room, we'll meet in heaven."

We have peculiar ideas about heaven being a sort of better-than-here place.

67

I saw this at one of those big men's restrooms at O'Hare Field in Chicago. All the automatic flushes in the urinals came on with lots of pressure, overflowed, and ran on the ground. Many men came running out of there still zipping up their pants. One of the funniest sights I have ever seen — but will it preach?

Humor Singing

A little boy in Northern Ireland was riding a bicycle and singing: "The Protestants got all the housing." A priest stopped and asked him to sing something different, like "Jesus was born in a stable." So the little lad rode away singing "Jesus was born in a stable, because the Protestants got all the housing."

What songs do we sing and what is the symbolism of them for others who hear them?

Hurt

Pastor David Rowe points out: "There is an old African proverb which says it doesn't matter whether the elephants are fighting or making love, the flowers still get trampled." While we discuss, debate, deliberate, let's look around and see the people who are being hurt.

*   *   *

Driving our church bus to Colorado where we all went whitewater rafting, I noticed that gophers would run out to the middle of the road, stand on their hind feet, look around, and then sometimes return. If they stopped and looked and turned back, they were often hit by the car or truck or a bus. It hurts to go back.

*   *   *

This evening I saw a hit-and-run accident at the corner of Keo and Ninth Street. An antique truck hit and knocked down a traffic light and drove on. Our lives are often strewn with the results of hit and run. Often we don't even know we have done the damage and caused the hurt as we go right on.

*   *   *

On this beautiful sunshining spring morning a bird flew into the kitchen window with a dramatic thud. The bird dropped to the ground stunned. After a while it regained its composure and flew away.

Sudden trauma comes in the middle of such nice times and God helps us recover and go on.

*   *   *

A young woman named Jennifer called at 1 a.m. to ask for help. She was in a phone booth on Grand Avenue with her little baby. She had been beaten badly by her husband. We got her a room for the night and took her to a store for some clothing the next day. The Christ would have us available to those who are hurt and are hurting.

Hymn

I was in our car, stopped at a traffic light in Berkeley. I noticed the couple next to me nodding their heads and tapping their hands to the same hymn tune I was listening to on a local religious FM station. It's always a joy to see others on the same wavelength as Christians.

Illusion

One time Carol Jarrett of Tiffin, Ohio, had a surprise birthday party for her husband, John. When we tried to cut the cake — it was cardboard. The baker had sold them the model in the case! Many attractive things are not what they appear on the outside.

Impersonation

The Ledger-Dispatch of Antioch, California, told a fascinating story of deception and impersonation. "Troy Smylie helped at a murder scene, assisted police taking suspects into custody, and even repaired an officer's gun." Smylie wasn't a cop — he has now been taken into custody, accused of masquerading as a police officer for more than a month and fooling even the real ones in San Francisco.

69

"The fraud came to light when Smylie walked into the police department's field operations bureau. An alert sergeant noticed the 35-year-old fit the description of a suspect who had been taking police vehicles and posing as an officer.

"The unemployed truck driver had found the badge on a city bus. He first wore the badge — then started hanging around the police service garage and befriending workers there. On one occasion the imitation cop responded to a murder scene helping out the real police officers.

"Smylie faces an array of accusations — stealing police cars, receiving stolen goods, burglary, and impersonating a police officer."

Incarnation

"Mama Ganna" (Amanda Gardner), the Bible Woman of Liberia, West Africa, said of the missionary nurse who raised and taught her, Marie Jensen, that when she taught, she "... wore Marie Jensen's skin." Since then many letters have arrived from my students there which have said, "Today I wore your skin ... I taught them about Jesus." Jesus put on our skin in the incarnation and asks us to wear his skin in the world in our ministry.

*　*　*

Father Taylor of Boston used to say: "There is just enough room in the world for all the people in it; but there is no room for the fences which separate them." — W. Barclay, *Commentary on Ephesians*.

*　*　*

A while back there were a number of letters to the editor of *The Lutheran* magazine about how to usher people in and out of church. Finally a letter came like this: "Usher them in, usher them out; I say lock the doors and see if they can live with each other!" Good point. Can we realize in the church the brotherhood and sisterhood we are always talking about?

*　*　*

Sir Philips Gibbs in his book *The Cross of Peace* wrote of modern civilization: "Modern progress has made the world a neighborhood. God has given us the task of making it a sisterhood and brotherhood. In the days of dividing walls of race and class and creed we must shake the earth anew with the message of the all-inclusive Christ, in whom there is neither bond or free, Jews or Greek ... but all in one."

*   *   *

I was seated on a plane today, wearing black suit and clerical collar. Ron Zalenski came to me and wanted to sit in the empty seat next to me. He had driven out from his home in Wisconsin to go hunting. His wife called to tell him their twenty-year-old son, Stephen, was in a car wreck, barely alive in hospital. They were Roman Catholics. Seeing me on flight, he asked, "Please, let me sit next to you. I'm afraid."

There is often a ministry of presence called for when words are of little use. Just be there and stay close.

*   *   *

In the made-for-television show, *Inside The Third Reich*, a little boy saw soldiers at the train station coming back from the front. So he slept on the hard floor in order to sympathize with them. After this discovery, the father said, "Son, I hope I can always remember how much I love you right now."

The God person comes incarnate to sympathize with the human existence.

*   *   *

Julie Walters, 34, an actress making the film *She'll Be Wearing Pink Pajamas,* announced during a nude scene that a new ruling by the Screen Actors Guild was that all technicians must also get nude during the filming. The naked truth was that it was a bluff; she told them after they had done it.

Jesus came to earth to strip down just like us and share what it's like to be fully human — it's called the incarnation.

71

*   *   *

When an orchestra plays, there is a "side man" who is not the lead musician but "sides" the lead musician. The "sideman" usually stands nearby the leader and supports the star by the way he or she plays the second part of the music.

Jesus is our "sideman." We are called to "side" each other. May the melody be great!

*   *   *

At the training camp for the Pittsburgh Pirates in Bradenton, Florida, there are four diamonds, a pitching machine, and a game going on with a junior college.

And there are the old retired players who suit up and mingle with the young active players in the dugout and behind home plate screen. They urge the younger ones on. So the incarnation when God suits up as Jesus, a human, and is with us.

Inclusiveness

"Springing up on Pentecost and Calvary, the church flows through the ages like a river, that same river and no other will flow unchangingly on through the ages until that great day when it will empty completely into the formed sea of eternal blessedness."
— Wilhelm Loehe, Neuendettelsau, Germany

*   *   *

"All the races of men have sprung from the same blood and thus have the same bloodline ... as I in my age am a drop of the great river, a member of the church, so am I a brother of the fathers who came before me and the children who came after me."
— Wilhelm Loehe

*   *   *

Just north of our church was Bethel Mission, a homeless shelter for "knights of the road." I was walking up there to hand out some hats on a cold January day when I saw "minorities," one a black, the other a white, helping a Native American into the mission door. All had been drinking. The Native American had a black garbage bag with all his possessions over his shoulder. He was new to the mission. The others were old-timers.

Why can't we do this welcoming of brothers and sisters well-dressed and sober?

*   *   *

In Lloyd C. Douglas's play about the Passion, there is a character who claims the crucifixion did more than demonstrate God's love, did more than save and forgive us. He said, "There was something about the man that made us into a tight little band of blood brothers and sisters." Someone has said, when asked, "Am I my brother's keeper?" that the answer is, "No, you are more than that. You are your brothers' brother and sisters' sister." Now, that will preach.

Inhumanity

In the televison special *Wallenberg*, a Lutheran Swede and member of a wealthy family in Sweden saved many Jews from the Nazis in Poland and Hungary. He said to his driver upon seeing a death march, "What shall we Christians say about this thing?" The driver answers, "I don't know, I'm not a theologian." Wallenberg responds, "Perhaps we are witnessing the death of God."

What horrible things we humans do to each other.

Jealousy

I saw the Shakespeare play *Othello* again. After suspicion is planted in Othello about Desdemona and Cassio, it eats him up and he kills out of misery and distrust. Jealousy is chief of the powers that work against God.

Jerusalem

All Bataks of Sumatra can tell you their *Bona Pinesa* (village of origin). Even if gone for years they return, visit, greet old friends, relatives, and family. No matter where they are in the world, they still have their village of origin. Many ballads are composed about it. Toba Bataks often return to Simasur Island of the Lake Toba area.

73

Our city of origin is Jerusalem, the place of our family of God, the place of Calvary, the empty tomb, and the Pentecost Spirit. Through worship and prayer let us return there.

Joy

A little sign on my desk says, "Joy is not the absence of trouble, but the presence of God." The great preacher George A. Buttrick used to say, "Joy is what we are chosen for and joy is what we have to offer to all who will come. It is a deep sense of joy not dependent on the number of things we got done in a day — for this is not the opposite of unhappiness but the opposite of unbelief."

* * *

In a church newsletter authored by friend/pastor Dan Johns was the story of Chippy the parakeet. Cleaning the cage one day, the owner was disturbed by the telephone and got the hose of the vacuum cleaner too close and sucked the bird right into the sweeper bag. Quickly she took the bag off, pulled out the bewildered bird, and stuck it under the water faucet. The bird survived, but now its owner describes it this way: "Chippy doesn't sing much any more, he just sits and stares."

Our church has many who don't sing much any more, but just sit and stare. How shall we minister God's loving grace and profound joy to them?

* * *

Mark Page, who donated a beautiful electronic organ for our seminary chapel, at its dedication said: "If it were possible for an organ to be happy, this one certainly is."

Happiness is elusive — what brings it to us, and is it important over the long haul?

* * *

I saw a sign hanging from a crane which said simply: "My Linda's O.K." What marvelous things we have to celebrate!

* * *

After riding a public bus for four hours, then walking about three miles back into the Sumatran jungle, we arrived at the *Bona Pinesa* (village of origin) of one of my Batak Christian Seminary students. After catechizing approximately 150 on Saturday evening, we drank coffee they had picked and roasted, and then we sang. A beautiful *Kebaya*-clad girl named Omega stood and lined out hymn after hymn to familiar tunes. The next morning I preached a naked, simple gospel: of Jesus born in Bethlehem, a ministry in Galilee, on the cross for our forgiveness, Easter resurrection that we too might come out of the grave, and return in spirit to be with us here and now. And then while the old women chewed *napuran*, we sang and sang and celebrated the presence of that same spirit with us still. A pig was killed and a *hula* (celebration) was held. We ate *sac sang* and they presented me an *ulas* (cloth of deep friendship). That simple, without-frills Christianity touched me deeply as we sang hymns of joy in God's presence. It was the basics at Tapiannauli bush village and it was full of joy.

Joy And Preaching

I preached in Curran Memorial Church in Sanoyea, Liberia, tonight. There were no lights in the church except for the ones the several hundred villagers brought with them. They placed a Coleman gasoline lantern in front of me so the congregation could see me as I spoke (no way to use notes or manuscript here!). The lantern kept running down and a deacon kept pumping it up during my sermon with the comment, "Preach on." We can bring light to those in darkness as we proclaim the Word.

After the service, and I had preached for an hour, the elder of the congregation led us through the town with lanterns and the Kpella choir dancing and playing sassas, drums, and animal horns tapped with a stick. Here is joy-filled, celebrated Christianity ... and to those who watched us that night there was no doubt about our joy in the Lord as we sang in the Kpella language: "Where are we going? We are going to God's Village."

75

Judge

The conductor of a community orchestra was upset because of poor attendance of musicians at the rehearsals. So he publicly thanked the one member who had not missed a rehearsal. The response was, "It's the least I could do since I won't be at the concert tonight."

Others' responses can be very disappointing but we must not judge them for it. Only God knows all their circumstances.

Leadership

Eric Gritch told of an Italian military captain leading a charge of soldiers. Sword forward, he jumped out of the trench and ran toward the enemy, shouting, "Avanti! Avanti!" From the trenches the soldiers shouted, "Bravo! Bravo!" but stayed in the trenches. He did a lonely charge cheered from behind.

There are different ways of leading and of following.

*   *   *

A boat going ahead of us smooths out the water for us to travel if we follow carefully. Following the Christ will not smooth our travel altogether, but it will help ... and we will not get lost along the way.

Life After Death

At the airport, there was a limo driver holding up a sign: "Katz." Others recognized family right away. They hugged and kissed and some even brought flowers to welcome home. When we come home to God we will be known. And the family of God will recognize us and welcome us there.

Life In Christ

Sometimes when there is a typhoon in the Phillippines some trees survive and are still standing, even with green leaves. But those who know will say, "That tree is already timber," meaning even though it doesn't look like it, it is dead. — an old man interviewed on CBS news.

We also can look like we are living but already dead. In the Christ there is new life.

Lifestyle

Alan Alda, in an interview about making movies, said that those now aged thirteen to 21 want three things: "Defy authority, destroy property, and take off clothes." How can God's people reach such an audience and how might we change their orientation toward a constructive lifestyle?

*　*　*

In an episode of television's *Cheers*, a fast-living Jack Dalton takes Sam and Diane for a ride in his airplane and fakes a heart attack. Thinking they are going to die, they tell each other how much they love each other; then they find he isn't dead at all.

Life can be more intense and we can be more sensitive and open when we became aware of its shortness.

*　*　*

At the Oakland airport I saw a car in the short-term parking lot with its motor running and two policemen trying to get in the locked doors to turn off the engine. I wonder what story was behind this picture? Just made the flight, but forgot to turn off the car? I believe we leave behind us all sorts of situations for others to solve (and many times don't realize we did it).

*　*　*

We live so fast! At O'Hare airport:

Hasty Pastry	Mexican in a Minute
Bun on the Run	Fast Far East
Pronto Pizza	Ice Cream Express
Lightning Lounge	

One of the gifts of Christian spirituality is to help people live on the run. It is also to set different values which help us slow down.

*　*　*

77

Carol left for church in a hurry. Our pet cat was on the roof of the station wagon. It dug its claws and tried to hang on but the faster the car went, the more the cat slid to the rear. At the bottom of Hanley Hill we all could see the cat's tail showing in the rear window of the wagon.

Our frantic lifestyle is similar. We try to hang on as we go faster and faster, losing ground all the time. There is a better way.

*   *   *

A couple closet comments: I had to sort out my neckties today. Some:

> Were outdated
> Will come back again
> Don't match my present wardrobe
> were designed for a specific occasion

I also had to do some shoe sorting:

> Hole in sole — comfortable but worn out
> Hurt when I wear now
> No longer in fashion
> Doctor said not good for me to wear

Perhaps we ought to sort our lifestyle, ways of doing things, values, priorities every so often in our Christian closet.

*   *   *

A Rolaids ad on television has Henry VIII saying the words, "Who is King around here? It's enough to give a man heartburn."

We can ask of our lifestyle and priorities: Who is the king around here? We have a savior-king waiting for our allegiance and service.

*   *   *

Andy Rooney on *60 Minutes* was looking through many travel brochures. He asked, "Why isn't it ever raining in any of these pictures? And there are never any crowds either. When you get there, everyone is dressed just like you."

We do romanticize life and often think it far better somewhere else.

On a warm day in the middle of one of Iowa's very cold winters, the road crews were out power washing the dirt and grime off the road signs. It probably got there by snowplows and salt trucks. We need be sure the grime of our daily routines is continually washed off the directional signs for our lives.

Light

On the 4th of July, I noticed during a fireworks display in Urbandale, Iowa, that one star in the heaven continued to shine brightly while all the human-made fireworks went off. After we humans have shot off our stuff, still God's light remains constant.

*   *   *

At the wedding of Jeff White and Leigh Smith at the Church of the Land, I turned and invited them to light the unity candle. No matches or tapers! A man with a Bic came out of the congregation and offered a light. How might we offer a light to marriages struggling to survive?

*   *   *

I heard the story of a new captain of a battleship. On his first cruise out of New York harbor he spotted a light ahead. He radioed ahead and said for the light to identify itself and take a 90 degree turn right. No response. He radioed again, "Look, I'm a battleship and can blow you out of the water. Take a 90-degree turn to the right." The response came back, "I'm the lighthouse and you take the 90 degree turn."

We have a light in the darkness to give us direction. We often try to move the lighthouse rather than alter our course. Now this will really preach.

*   *   *

John Stossel on *20/20* reported about SAD (seasonal affective disorder) syndrome. A new cure is to furnish full spectrum lights two hours per day. This helps overcome the depression. So can the light of Christ for those who still live in darkness. The way it works is that to overcome the short daylight of winter days, the artificial light goes into the brain and stops the brain from releasing the chemical melatonin — which also causes us to sleep at night.

Living Parables

At our annual staff Christmas party our little Sarah's turn had come to relate her most memorable Christmas. She said it was when we came upon a car accident on the way to Grandmother's house and Carol and I got blood on ourselves trying to help. I had expected her to describe toys she had always wanted or something like that.

Doing good to the person in the ditch is still recommended.

Lost And Found

My outboard motor, which had been stolen, was repurchased in a sting operation by the police and I now have it back. My motor has now been twice purchased. So too me. Once purchased through my baptism and again on the cross.

*   *   *

At the Dallas/Fort Worth airport, I saw a bag falling off the baggage cart on the way to an airplane. A supervisor finally came out, placed a red tag on it, and took it to the conveyor loading a plane for the same destination. We were lost and we have been found by the Christ who puts us on our way to our correct destination again.

*   *   *

I saw an old man in the hot parking lot of the hospital. He had lost his car while visiting his wife. I drove him all around the lot but he did not recognize it. When I looked at his ticket, I discovered he was in the wrong lot. We went to the other side of the hospital and there it was. He probably had come out of a different door than he had entered.

There are so many lost in the heat, frustration, and confusion of our lives. We must invite them to come over to the other side.

Love

On the sitcom *Night Court*, Dan Fielding was in the hospital, close to death, and had partially recovered. Fielding said, "In order to love, one must be able to give — so no one will love me because I can't give. I love you, Harry. There, I said it." Harry replied, "Yeah, you said it. Now why don't you say it again to yourself."

Jesus tells us to love one another. We must also love one another as one of God's family whom God treasured.

*   *   *

In the movie *Starman*, an alien crash-lands right into the life of a widow. He hears her use the word "love" and asks her to define it. She replies, "Love is when you care more for someone else than you do for yourself." Jenny came very close to defining God's love which we have for another.

Luther

Today is Saint Martin's Day (Nov. 11), when Martin Luther was baptized at the age of one day in Saints Peter and Paul Church in Eisleben, Germany. A swan stands in his birth house nearby to remind us of Jan Hus, who was 100 years ahead of Luther and said before being burned at the stake for heresy, "You can cook this old goose, but a gander will come you cannot silence." In many places in the world (like South America) the swan is a symbol of Lutheranism.

Materialism

On the CBS news with Dan Rather, Bill Moyers said regarding the twenty-fifth anniversary of the Peace Corps, "We carry two passports. One is American and the other is human being." Let's never let the former block out the latter.

Maturity

In the television sitcom *Cheers*, his girlfriend says to Sam Malone, who tries to keep everyone happy and not get engaged, "You have to make some choices and commitments in your life, Sam — it's called growing up."

So, too, the Christian life, as we mature, we often must decide for or against. We must also decide whom we will serve and to whom we will commit our energy and resources.

Mercy

After a day of doing calls, counseling, meetings, and so forth, I removed my black suit coat only to discover a sheet of softener stuck to my shirt sleeve (from our dryer). Was it softer and gentler for those I ministered to and with that day?

*   *   *

"He likes me," little Elizabeth said after I put my hands on her head and blessed her at the communion rail while giving her parents Holy Communion.

The meal acts that out — God likes us ... and more.

*   *   *

A bumper sticker in Mercy Hospital said, "Take me to Mercy." In the Christ, God's mercy has come to us!

*   *   *

On the television show *Hill Street Blues*, Andy Renko said to Bobby Hill after freezing up in a crisis, "Just because I made this one mistake, you can't cancel every other thing I've done right up till now."

There is a wideness in God's mercy which ought to encourage a wideness in our mercy for others.

Ministry

There is a Mexican gardener at the Lutheran Center in Mexico City named Isidro Santiago who catechized his own five children and then presented them to the church for membership. He took Martin Luther seriously about the "priesthood of all believers."

*   *   *

When Bishop Wayne Weissenbuehler of Denver spoke to the Invitation to Service event at California Lutheran University, he told this story:

An Episcopal Bishop signaled for the acolyte to bring a pitcher of water and pour over his hands before communion. "Wait a minute," the Bishop said. "This isn't water; this is wine." The acolyte promptly replied, "It was water when I put it in there."

May the water of our baptism turn into wine of our ministry (vocation).

*   *   *

After 32 years of marriage, Dick and Jane called on their wedding anniversary to thank their pastor for helping them stay together those many years ago when their marriage was going apart. With three young children they were struggling, and a parish pastor counseled them. They wanted to say thanks 32 years later.

How many lives are enriched by parish ministry and we really never know it. But the spirit knows.

*   *   *

Nelvin Vos says, "... ministry is not something we go and do; rather it is something you do as you go." I like that. Each day, whatever our work, study, play, living at home experiences, gives us opportunity to do ministry.

*   *   *

In the construction of Park Place, a seventeen-story apartment complex, I noticed there was a relay man standing on the top of the structure relaying the instructions from the ground to the man operating the crane. A pastor sometimes has the awesome responsibility of relaying a person's message to God through prayer and also confession.

*   *   *

In the drama, *Mass Appeal*, young Deacon Dalson, priest in training, says to the older Father Farley after watching him compromise and do a song and dance in the pulpit: "What you believe is much more important than what your people think of you." Later Farley stops in the midst of confession and says, "My

83

need to be loved by you has gotten in the way of my telling you the truth." Real ministry insight.

* * *

At the Jack and Jill supermarket where I asked for a copy of *The National Enquirer*, the woman said at the checkout counter, "Father, you don't want to read that kind of smut!" I wanted the paper to see the account of Roger Williams' wedding in which I had participated. Look at this double standard. We clergy must live up to those high standards but also encourage the laity to do the same.

Miracle

In small discussion groups on miracles, some questioned whether there really were any. A wife of a recovering alcoholic responded: "I don't know why you find these miracles so hard to believe. I saw beer turned into furniture in my own home."

* * *

At the Cathedral of the Virgin of Guadalupe in Mexico, there is a long narthex hall full of hand-painted plaques representing the miracles occurring in individual lives. An example is a picture of a boat on fire, or a car hitting a pedestrian, or a person getting out of a hospital bed.

What miracles of our members could we paint on the walls of our church narthexes?

* * *

A Pan Am flight crashed in a severe thunderstorm just after takeoff from New Orleans Airport. Sheriff Lee found an eighteen-month-old baby in the debris who was still alive with everyone else killed. She was called by the media "Melissa, the miracle baby."

We have a miracle baby in Mary's son, Jesus in Bethlehem.

* * *

Del Monico told on radio: A man seated in a wheelchair at the Vatican suddenly got up and walked away. Everyone was amazed and shouted and praised God for a miracle. But the man hadn't been ill. He was just resting for a little but in a vacant chair.

God is accustomed to doing miracles every day and they appear quite commonplace. On the other hand, some things which seem miraculous just aren't explainable yet. God most often works within God's own natural law.

* * *

"Florida city drained by Virgin Mary pilgrimage."

An article in the *Contra Costa Times* newspaper of January 5, 1997, claimed that in Clearwater, Florida, the crowds coming to see an image resembling the Virgin Mary on a glass office building are costing the city big bucks.

"The faithful have numbered 450,000 — four and one half times the city's population — over the three weeks since the image was first noticed. And a city report put the tab at $40,000 to deploy police to handle the crowds and direct traffic." The document also tells of easily riled worshipers and votive candles that started fires, including one that burned a police officer.

"A city panel dubbed the Miracle Management Task Force decided to scale back crowd and traffic control efforts over the weekend.

"Meantime, the image is still on the side of the Seminole Finance building and its owners have no plans to try to remove it."

Mission

Dennis Anderson, President of Trinity Lutheran Seminary in Columbus, Ohio, told of a woman named Judy Cobb of West Virginia who claimed, "We must rediscover the theology of go." Like Paul and Muhlenberg and Father Hyer.

* * *

Bishop David Brown reminded the Iowa District of the American Lutheran Church of Moltmann's words: "... the church is because of mission, not mission because of the church."

We often get that backwards. Because there is a mission of gospel witness and discipleship, we organize to do the mission.

It's not that we do the mission to protect, serve, and so forth, the church.

*   *   *

I visited the memorial for Henry Lyman and Samuel Munson, missionaries from the United States who were killed by the Batak in Sumatra. One of the old farmers nearby joked he had missionary blood in his family because his ancestors had eaten two of them! It was the year 1843. In that same year a baby boy was born in Germany named Ingar Ludwig Nommensen who became the famous "Apostle to the Bataks" and is still considered the father of Christian missions in Sumatra. He served in Sumatra for 65 years as a Christian missionary. Even at times when it seems all is lost in the church, God is moving to call new leadership to establish the Kingdom.

Music

Today I did not preach so I could see from my pew in the chancel our organist, Linda Wibben, actually practicing on the organ console for the next hymn during the sermon. Her hands were just flying on the keyboard with no music coming out of the instrument.

Preparation for life's struggles ahead of time can help when they come. What hymns shall we practice for the days ahead? "O God our help in ages past." "On our way rejoicing." "A mighty fortress is our God." "My faith looks up to thee."

Offering

In an Iowa snowstorm the willow trees in back of our home bent way over from the weight. The sun came out and melted off the load and the pliable trees straightened up again. Storms come, the Son melts away the heavy load, and we straighten up again.

Ordination

We ordained 41 that hot Sunday morning in the church in Medan, Sumatra. First a short parade to the church led by a band of fourteen, then preaching, speeches, and the ordination of pastors, deaconesses, teachers/preachers, Bible women, evangelists, and elders of the church. The Bataks recognize six different kinds of ministries. After more speeches, including mine, we sat on the front pews and celebrated with a roasted pig, rice, sac sang, and greens all eaten with our hands. There was a loud din of picture taking, shouting, music, food being consumed, and warm greetings and congratulations. It seemed right that the new ministries began with a deep sense of joy.

Our Soul

Rolly Martinson tells the story of a boy who would not stop clicking his heels each time he stood up in church. His father finally pushed him down with his hand on his head. The boy said, "You may have shoved me to where I'm sitting down on the outside; but I am still standing up on the inside." Perhaps how the outside looks doesn't tell what the inside images.

Overburdened

A truck driver going through a town on the truck route stopped at each stop street, got out, banged on the side of the truck with a ball bat, got back in and drove on. When asked why this strange procedure, he explained: "I have a two-ton truck and four tons of canaries aboard, and I have to keep two tons in the air all the time."

We, too, are overloaded and instead of facing the reality, we rearrange the load. — Frank Harrington

Parables

January 21, 1991: Helicopters and fighter planes left the security of their air bases to fly into enemy territory in order to rescue just one downed pilot. It's like the story Jesus told of a shepherd who left the field to rescue just one lost sheep.

*   *   *

A pastor preaching in Charlotte, North Carolina, said, "There are three basic attitudes reflected in the parable of the Good Samaritan:
1) What's yours is mine and I'll take it.
2) What's mine is mine and I'll keep it.

87

3) What's mine is yours and I'll share it.
Nice twist on the text. It will preach.

Parenthood
Letty Cottin Pogrebia in *Growing Up*: "Don't be the man you think you should be, be the father you wish you had."

Parenthood is an awesome responsibility and a Godly act.

Pastor
In my childhood my pastor, Christian Wessel, was like a father to me. I adored him. While fishing in the Greenville, Ohio, park lagoon, the day after they stocked it for the boy scout fishing contest and a day before the boy scouts arrived, he waded into the water waist-deep to retrieve a fishing pole being dragged by a fish. He then stood on the bank, took off his pants, and wrung them out. I remember thinking to myself: "Look, he wears underwear like I do!" It was one of the signs to this little boy that I too would be a pastor.

Peace
At the Augustana-Hochschule (Seminary) in Neuendettelsau, Germany, I was told that the facilities now used by that school were a large ammunition factory during the Third Reich, with workers living in what is now the dormitory and generals living in what are now the faculty homes. The Nazis placed it there, close to hospitals and homes for orphans and elderly, in hopes Americans would not bomb it.

Now there is swords into plowshares!

*   *   *

At the installation of a chaplain to the homeless at People's Park in Berkeley, the invitation was extended to offer the peace to each other. A large black dog snapped at a man who kicked it in the teeth.

Peace seems so temporary, artificial, and elusive.

*   *   *

At the Bishop's conference at Livermore lab today with theologians and scientists, the Bishop said, "After all, the fact is we are all determined to protect our things and hang on to them with our nuclear weapons, even if we destroy ourselves in the meantime."

"Blessed are the peacemakers," said Jesus.

* * *

In the movie *Sacrifice*, the African woman says, "I just want peace. I want to come home to kindness again. I'll fight with you, but don't ask me to kill." We Christians have the great gift of peace and the great task of peacemaking.

* * *

A news item in *U.S. News and World Report*: the weight of heavy snow has exploded some 1500 of the mines placed along East Germany's border with West Germany. — February 15, 1982, issue.

Many under the weight of their daily life are about to explode. Or is this God's way of saying "no" to maiming other human beings?

* * *

There is a beautiful scene in the television movie *The Scarlet and the Black*, when Monsignor O'Flaherty of the Holy See in Rome finally baptized General Kaplan of the German SS after World War II. After visiting the general every week for a long time, O'Flaherty baptized his former bitter enemy in 1959. Kaplan hated the monsignor because he helped prisoners of war escape. Only our Christian faith can turn enemies into friends like this.

* * *

I asked Dr. Bernard Spinard, nuclear scientist at Iowa State University, how much peaceful energy is stored up in a nuclear warhead. He said one warhead would have enough energy to run all of Iowa for 48 years at present level of consumption.

Pragmatic reason for turning pruning hooks into plowshares.

*   *   *

In the liturgy of the Jewish bat mitzvah of Julie and Valerie Glauberg was this beautiful prayer: "In a world torn by pain, a world far from wholeness and peace, a world waiting still to be redeemed, give us, Lord, the courage to say: 'There is one God in heaven and earth.' "

*   *   *

Aboard the space shuttle *Discovery* an Arab prince asked about trouble between countries responded, "They should see the world from up here — it looks a lot different. There aren't any political lines drawn." God must see us that way also. In fact, drawing the political lines may be an insult to our createdness.

*   *   *

"Every gun that is made, every warship launched, every rocket fired signifies in the final sense a theft from those who hunger and are not fed, those who are cold and are not clothed. This world of arms is not spending money alone. It is spending the sweat of its laborers, the genius of its scientists, the hopes of its children ... this is not a way of life at all in the true sense. Under the cloud of threatening war, it is humanity hanging from a cross of Iron." —Dwight D. Eisenhower, from a speech before the American Society of Newspaper editors, 1953.

Peacemaker
I saw on the news tonight Bishop Tutu dressed in a purple cassock wading into a rioting crowd in South Africa. They were beating a man whom they then intended to burn. He waded right in and saved the man's life!

"Blessed are the peacemakers."

Penance
In Bavaria the Christians observe in November a day called *Bustag* (a day of penance). The custom comes from years ago and the Old Testament idea of the king having subjects do a day of *Buse* (penance) when the country was threatened. It is held ten

days before Advent begins and always on a Wednesday. At Wittenberg it is each night for the ten nights before Advent. Oh, how we Americans could use the idea of repentance, and penance.

Pentecost

That first Pentecost must have been something else! 3000 baptized. Pity the poor altar guild who prepared the font and think of the church secretary who had to get all the certificates in order. The usher must have had quite a time parking the chariots and camels. The property committee probably rebelled at cleaning up the parking lot after that long service. The acolyte had to hold 3000 burning candles. That next week when the other Jerusalem pastors met for text study, they were heard saying, "Yes, but the theology is weak there, and besides they probably will go out the back door as fast as they came in the front."

*   *   *

The local parish church was on fire and a crowd gathered. The pastor spotted an inactive member and commented: "Joe, this is the first time I have seen you at church for a long time." Joe responded, "Well, Pastor, this is the first time I have seen this church on fire!" Yes — let the Pentecost fire set our congregations ablaze!

*   *   *

While driving across Iowa from Iowa City to Des Moines, I observed many little grass fires along the railroad track. They had been started in some way by a train's engine. I also saw many fire trucks on their way to extinguish the fires. But the engineer proceeded along, starting fires in his wake. I'll bet we do that in life's journey also!

Potential

Mark Twain tells the story of the Calaveras County jumping frog. Angels Camp, a gold mining frontier town has a monument and annual frog jumping contest to this day. The famous jumping frog of Calaveras County finally lost the contest because it was fed heavy shot.

What are we fed which weighs us down and keeps us from being all we are created to be?

*   *   *

Henri Nouwen told of a little boy seeing a great sculptor at work. He asked, "How did you know there was a lion in that piece of marble?" Who knows what is inside us. Only God is able to see all the wonderful possibilities.

Power

Pastor Joe Allison of Saint Peters, Monrovia, Liberia, tells that after 600 were slaughtered in the sanctuary of his church, the group decided to worship in the Lutheran Church in Liberia guest house area. Just as Pastor Allison was about to pronounce the benediction, armed troops broke through the wall's gate and headed toward their little congregation. Allison said, "Everyone, hold your Bible in front of your head, shout the word 'Jesus,' and follow me." They marched out of there with Bibles and "Jesus." The soldiers parted to let them through, not one raising his gun against them. There is still power in the name of Jesus.

*   *   *

A man by the name of William Quinn is in jail in San Francisco right now, accused of sending letter bombs. He is supposed to have planted explosives in a hollowed-out Bible. The Bible can be that explosive without humans stuffing it with dynamite. (The root word for dynamite is *dinimus*, used a number of times in the New Testament.) Loving neighbor and enemy, going the second mile, turning the other cheek, forgiving seventy times is indeed radical and explosive!

*   *   *

I had an intern nicknamed "Crash Adrian." She drove church vans. She once crashed one into the other in our church lot. (We do hurt our own.)

Also, a van developed a power steering leak and would only turn right, not left. She had to figure out her route from Walgreen's

92

while turning only right. She did it by backing up a couple of times. There are times when we ought back up and go the other way. Perhaps we should examine our "power steering" also. What powers it and how reliable is it for us?

*   *   *

In Joe Wold's book *God's Impatience with Liberia* (p. 104), Louis Bowers went across the Saint Paul River to the village of Parakwele. There, fourteen men were ready to be baptized by the local Evangelists. The Zo stood up and said, "I forbid these men to be baptized. If they are, by this time tomorrow they will be dead." The men went outside for a *palaver*. They came back and said, "We will be baptized; if we die we will be with Jesus." When the service was over, the Zo came to Bowers secretly and said, "Tell me about this Jesus. His power is greater than mine."

How does one describe the power of Jesus?

*   *   *

We almost always underestimate the power of the wind. I followed a truck today with its canvas flapping in the wind. You see it whenever humans try to tie down a cover on anything and then move it — or the wind comes up.

We almost always underestimate the Spirit's power as well. Let Pentecost blow!

*   *   *

In order to install cable for television in a trench, the utility company has to come out and mark where electric, gas, and telephone wires are buried. They use little red flags; the trench for the cable can then be dug. As we mature as Christians we need to mark where the power for our lives is, as well as the dangers.

*   *   *

In the movie *Schindler's List*, Schindler is on the balcony of the home of the commandant of a prison camp where for sport the commandant would shoot prisoners walking in the prison yard. Schindler said to him, "Real power is when you have the power to shoot them if you want to, but you do not." When we have the power to get even and do not is when God's power of love and forgiveness is most real.

Prayer

From Robert Fulghum's book, *Uh-Oh*: "A Hudson Bay start meant the frontiersmen always camped the first night a few short miles from the company headquarters. This allowed the gear and supplies to be tried out, so if anything had to be kept behind it was still easy to return. A thoughtful beginning spared the travelers later difficulty."

A prayerful beginning to each day's journey will also make the trip go better equipped all day.

*　　*　　*

In a historical museum along the Mississippi River in Iowa, there is a sign at the helm of an old riverboat which reads: "In a storm pray toward heaven but row toward shore." There are times to pray and times to act on the prayer and actually become the way God answers it.

*　　*　　*

I took the large bag of rice into the Brewersville refugee camp for little Carol Kollie's family who survived the murder of her father and brothers in Degei town. Her mother said she had prayed the night before that somehow God would help her with providing rice for her children or she would end her life herself. Then I showed up with the prayed-for rice. I was the instrument through which God had answered the prayer of a desperate Liberian woman. We are often the channel through which God answers the prayer of God's people.

*　　*　　*

Katherine Brownfield, who sends me humor, sent this one. A man frequently prayed this prayer in prayer meeting: "O God, clean out the cobwebs from my mind." One night, a woman followed the

94

man in prayer and prayed thus: "O God, don't clean out the cobwebs. Kill the spider!"

We often fail to get to the source of our problem and only consider the symptoms.

*   *   *

Katherine Brownfield also sent me this gem:

A little boy was asked in Bible School to memorize the Lord's Prayer. Sitting on the floor in the living room, head bowed and chubby hands folded, he reverently said: "Our Father, who art in heaven, how did you know my name?"

God knows us by name, each one, as God knows every sparrow which falls from the heavens.

*   *   *

I was in O'Hare airport dressed in my black clericals when a young man with a bottle of champagne came to me and asked that I pray for his wife who was having a baby in an Oakland Hospital. She flew out there because she wanted the doctor who delivered her as a baby to deliver her first child. This father was scared. He knelt and I prayed as it got very still around us. The first-time father didn't care who the person was in clergy dress — he just wanted a prayer right then.

Perhaps we ought to be more public about our calling rather than trying to fit into this increasingly secular society. Our ministries may be increasingly for those who have little or no knowledge of church.

*   *   *

Peter Narum told me about a flood. It was up to the first floor the first day and a boat came and offered to remove the homeowner from the home. The answer was: "No, I trust God."

The second day, water was to the second floor and the boat offered to help. Same response: "No, I trust God."

The third day the man was on the roof and the water was still rising. A helicopter came to help. "No, I trust God."

95

In Heaven now, the man said to God, "I trusted you; why didn't you help?" God answered, "I tried; I sent two boats and a helicopter."

God often sends answers to our prayers through others.

*   *   *

On NBC's made-for-television show, *Going Home*, Bobby is dying of cancer and asked his father, "What's going to happen to me when I die? Where will I go?" The father replied, "Son, I don't know." Bobby said, "Grandpa knows, he talks to God." Grandpa said after finding out Bobby was dying: "You think tears dry up when you get old? Everything dries up but that!"

Life here hurts, but those who speak to God get through.

*   *   *

In the television special *September Gun*, Ben Sunday, a gunfighter, tells a nun, "The secret of good baked beans is to be hungry as hell" and "When you shoot, pray; when they shoot, duck."

There are times to pray and times to act. A combination of both is probably the best: action and prayer.

*   *   *

The pastor was visiting in the parlor. A young farm boy had just killed a big rat and came running into the room to tell his mother, "... and I stamped and stamped on it," then, noticing the pastor for the first time, added, "... and God called it home."

We often have one language for the church and another for the world, and fail to connect the two.

*   *   *

Lyndon Johnson, President of the United States, asked Bill Moyers to offer prayer at the White House (Moyers is a former Baptist minister). He started very softly, so LBJ said, "Speak up, Bill." Moyers replied without ever looking up: "I wasn't speaking to you, Mr. President." Our prayers often are spoken for other people to hear rather than God.

*   *   *

I noticed a large satellite dish at Archer television today. It was moving to adjust to a signal from a satellite. I believe we must often re-adjust our reception direction in order to hear God speak to us.

* * *

A female patient in the hospital today said to me after a radical breast removal for cancer: "I prayed to God not to let this happen to me — but he (*sic*) didn't hear me."

Because God doesn't answer our prayer request doesn't mean he doesn't hear them.

Preaching

A woman who had dated a divorced United Methodist minister several times shot the 36-year-old pastor dead in front of his congregation in the first moments after he finished a sermon on "bringing home the harvest of God's love."

Elizabeth S. Mayberry of Bloomington, Indiana, was charged with murder in the shooting death of Roland Phillips, Jr., pastor of North Salem United Methodist Church, located north of Indianapolis.

Mayberry walked down the center aisle and approached the pulpit, saying she had to speak with him. Phillips asked Mayberry to wait until he had finished the sermon, and she stood next to him for several minutes as he concluded. After the preacher finished, a song was announced. At that point Mayberry pulled out the pistol and gunned the pastor down. — *Christian Century*, October 13, 1993.

Many a preacher died in the pulpit trying to preach!

* * *

At an assembly of Lutheran pastors at Asilomar in California, an artist from Nebraska by the name of Marxhausen told the assembled group: "I don't teach students to draw. I teach them to see."

We must as preachers learn to see so we can paint homiletical pictures in the pulpit.

97

*   *   *

I attended an ecumenical service today at Saint John's Catholic Church in Des Moines. After being seated I discovered that two pillars holding up the sanctuary roof completely blocked my view of the pulpit. I wonder what church pillars block the message from the pulpit? Traditions, heresies, wrong perceptions, our own pride ...?

*   *   *

I have been chasing the ghost of a nineteenth century preacher here in Neuendettelsau, Germany. Wilhelm Loehe was pastor here for 35 years and in that time revived the diaconal movement providing women to serve in institutions of mercy here and in other locations. He sent missionaries to three continents and began many hospitals, homes for mentally disadvantaged, orphans, delinquent boys, schools, homes for unwed mothers, and so forth. In chasing his ghost I found his greatness in preaching (often called "the Chrysostom of his century") can be ascribed to the following suggestions:

1. A strong confident voice is important.
2. The preacher's own witness is crucial to the effectiveness of the proclamation.
3. Keep the message simple so it is understandable by all.
4. Work to move the heart and senses as well as intellect.
5. Use the familiar story, metaphor, personification.
6. Paint word pictures, including smell and taste.
7. Find new ways to present the old truths with strong imagination.
8. Break loose from the manuscript and talk directly to the people.
9. Preaching for results — always answering the "so what?" question.
10. Enlist the advice of others in preparation and critique of delivery.
11. See that the entire liturgy supports the sermon.
12. An exciting congregational ministry and mission will help produce exciting preaching and vice versa.

Precious

During Nikita Khrushchev's visit to the U.S. he bought material for a new suit. When he got home he was told there was not enough to make the suit.

When Khrushchev protested, the tailor told him: "... but you are not as big a man in the U.S. as in Russia."

Our greatness is of little consequence as we move to other surroundings, but being purchased with the blood of Christ makes us precious wherever we are.

Prejudice

A pastor told of having old church records of a Norwegian congregation which listed membership as: "52 souls and 2 Swedes."

Something in our very genes keeps us narrower than we ought to be.

*   *   *

I followed a large cement truck being towed up Lower Beaver Road. I wondered what happens when a truck full of concrete stalls and the barrel no longer rotates. I drove on out to the concrete place to ask. They carry a certain chemical with them just in case, and they can put it in the mix to keep it from setting up in the barrel of the truck.

What might we use to keep our minds and prejudices from setting up like concrete?

Priorities

When the Berkeley Hills fire spread, Carol and I parked our station wagon, ready to leave in a minute if we needed to do so. The decision of what to take along was fascinating. I chose my old antique rifles, the donor computer disc, the crucifix given to me in Central America, and my Muhlenberg Bible box. Carol went right for the family pictures. What things are most important to us or represent what is most important in our lives? We need a time every so often when we identify the precious in our lives.

*   *   *

99

Our son was diagnosed with terminal cancer this week. He went for a second opinion right away. Perhaps we ought to provide second opinions for:

>getting what's coming to you
>demanding your rights
>staking out your turf
>we are all trying to go to the same place
>it was his time to go, and so forth

Prison

I purchased three goldfish for our fountain. When I let them out, two swam in a tight little circle as if still in the plastic bag. One really went for it and swam all around from side to side.

Sometimes we remain confined by our own lack of risk-taking.

Promise

The radio and television ads in Des Moines for Reichardt's clothing store have owner Bill say: "No sale is ever final here. We'll see you are completely satisfied here. I will see to it myself, because I'm here — I'm Bill Reichardt and I own the store." In the incarnation the creator of all promises us that our lives are secure. God never throws us out or away. The owner of the store is here with us and we have God's promise.

*   *   *

At the La Quinta Inn in Arvada, Colorado, two mallard ducks were sitting on the blue canvas covering the swimming pool. Their landing must have been a riot!

Things are not always as promising as they appear.

Recall

Five people died in Chicago from taking Tylenol Extra Strength. They found it was laced with poison.

There are many things presented as attractive and good for us (and will even help make us feel better) which are laced with the poison of sinfulness. Perhaps we ought to do a "recall" from our pulpits.

Reconciliation

The headline in the *Contra Costa Times*, November 16, 1997, read, "Family of slain Palestinian boy donates organs." An Associated Press story out of Jerusalem said that a nine-year-old Palestinian boy had died four days after an Israeli soldier shot him with a rubber-coated bullet. In a gesture of reconciliation his family donated their son's organs to needy people regardless of whether they were Israeli or Palestinian.

In a four-hour procedure, the child's heart, liver, kidneys, and lungs were removed and sent to a hospital outside Tel Aviv. "Authorities were preparing to quell unrest after today's funeral."

The shooting came after a group of boys threw stones at soldiers near the Jewish enclave of Rachel's Tomb on the outskirts of Bethlehem. Those parents taught many a lesson about reconciliation.

* * *

A television newscaster, Terilyn Joe, told the story of a San Francisco Japanese woman who is returning Japanese flags to their families. The flags were carried by Japanese soldiers during World War II. American soldiers took them off dead bodies for souvenirs. All the soldiers' families had signed them for good luck. Now they were returning them to the families, who are moved and thrilled to have them back. The Japanese families have written thank you letters and sent gifts of appreciation to the Americans. How about that for reconciliation?

Renewal

In Harry DeCarlo's restaurant in Des Moines, I noticed a box of Twix candy bars with the following sign: "Fresh before 1984."

Perhaps we ought to give out baptismal, first communion, or confirmation certificates with a similar sign which would remind us of our regular need for spiritual renewal and revival.

Rescue

CNN called John Freese, of the American Embassy in Liberia, a hero. He drove a military personnel carrier into Monrovia during the thick of the civil and tribal war and rescued a number of Americans, bringing them back to the Embassy where they were airlifted to Sierra Leone. Our task is not so much to rescue, as Jesus has done that. Our task is to take the "rescuer" out of the fortress and into the streets of the world to do and be in mission.

Rest

During a four-hour ordination service in the Batak Church in Medan, Sumatra, I saw the assistant to the Bishop, who had been working to pull it all together, go and squat on his haunches behind the altar to rest. There he was, in long black preaching gown with white tabs, squatted on the floor, resting like men do in their villages of origin back in the bush. Rest at God's altar. Perhaps we ought to preach more about the holy rest God gives at the table of the Lord. It's an important part of the gospel: a deeper *shalom*, a divine pause for rest.

Resurrection

Sam Donaldson on the ABC news told of Yellowstone Park, which burned last summer. It is now covered with a foot of snow. Underneath grass is starting to take root and seventy percent of the trees will survive. The heat of fire provides a gum which protects the pinecones. Two weeks later there is a shower of seeds that will start new pine trees. This is called "nature's fire insurance." It's new life out of destruction. A lived-out resurrection!

*   *   *

From Margaret in Forest City, Iowa:

A woman died and went to heaven, which was more beautiful than she'd ever expected. She couldn't wait to show it to her husband when he arrived, because he was an eternal pessimist.

A year later her husband joined her, and she took him on a tour. "The sky, the flowers, the music, the people — heaven is truly heaven, isn't it?" she explained. He surveyed Paradise briefly, then said, "Sure. And if it weren't for you and your darned oat bran, we'd have been here five years sooner!"

Could it be we avoid death too much? If paradise is really paradise, what is it we so fear?

*   *   *

August 7, 1994, Dean and Ruth Fardahl dropped off their lunch partners at Lord of Life Lutheran Church in Sun City West and headed home. A few blocks from home, Dean's heart stopped and he ran the car across the boulevard, into a yard, and into the side of a garage. Ruth was all right with some bruises. They rushed Dean to the hospital where the doctor told me that the airbag had opened and slammed into Dean's chest and started his heart again. I visited him the next day in Boswell Hospital in Sun City, where he was sitting up on the side of the bed dangling his feet.

Oh, to start the dead hearts again — inside and outside our congregations. It's an Easter story.

*   *   *

From my study window I can see the orange reflection of the sun in the morning in the windows of an insurance building long before it actually comes over the horizon to be seen. Easter is like seeing in Jesus' resurrection our own security long before we can view the physical proof of God's infinite care at our death or the death of our loved ones.

*   *   *

At the funeral of Ruth Walthall, Pastor William Zimman told of falling asleep on a trip as a child and waking up the next morning in his own bed. Heaven must be a similar experience.

*   *   *

I noticed today a bean sprout which had grown through the window (crack in the sill). It was beginning to die. I think it was now too far from its roots. It also had grown outside the sunshine's reach.

It's a warning for us. We must keep in contact with our roots and always where the light of Christ can nourish our being.

103

*   *   *

There are several scenes in the movie *Cocoon* which speak of new life. Bernie tries to take his dead wife into the pool and Walter says: "It's too late, Bernie, the life is gone." Sin is pictured when one regressed into being unfaithful to his wife again. Life in the water — a beautiful picture of baptism and the new life we have in Christ.

*   *   *

In the Batak culture of Sumatra, Indonesia, there is a strong custom of *tugu*. After ten years the family must build an elaborate tomb and move the dead bones of their ancestors to it. The ceremony is expensive and costly to the families of the poor. To apply our resurrection theology to this custom, Christian families gather at the *tugu* on Easter eve, stay all night, and then gather in their churches early Easter morning to celebrate the resurrection of Jesus Christ. Somehow their actions say that a tomb, no matter how elaborate, will not do it. It's the promise of Easter which takes us through. Bataks also have a saying: *Ndang marimba tano hamatean.* Translated this means: "Any burial place in the world is acceptable." Our dwelling place shall be in heaven. The *tugu* is empty.

Resurrection And Death

Atlanta's Dion James hit a ball in Shea Stadium which hit and killed a dove on the fly. He got a double and thus set it up for the Braves to win the game. A fly ball to left field had been turned into a double. It was the first time ever in Major League baseball. Shortstop Rafael Santana had to pick up the dead bird and bring it to the bat girl, who didn't want it.

Life is as fickle for us as for the bird. Death comes any time. Our finest efforts can kill.

Revenge

In an exposé on television about Sobibor (*sic*), an Eastern Poland death camp, a Jew commented, "Yes, we work for them.

104

We survive for one reason — revenge. God will forgive us. Some are wondering if we can ever forgive God?" — aired April 12, 1987.

It is possible to live our lives mainly motivated by hate.

* * *

I saw a rerun of the film *Gandhi*.

A Hindu man came to him and confessed he had killed a Moslem boy. Gandhi said he knew a way out of his hell. Find a parentless boy and raise him as a Moslem.

"When we follow 'an eye for an eye' we end up with a world which cannot see." —Gandhi

* * *

Two Jews went to synagogue on Yom Kippur. They hated each other. Now all is forgiven. They came out the door and one said to the other: "I wish for you all you wish for me." The other replied, "You're starting it again!" — told by George Forell at field seminary in Tucson, Arizona.

How easy it is to harbor a grudge and nurse a hurt rather than do the hard work of radical forgiveness.

* * *

A town put on the passion play and recruited a non-Christian to play the part of Jesus Christ. While carrying the cross, the crowd taunted him and he attacked them the very first night. After further coaching he just gritted his teeth and said: "Okay for now, but just wait until the resurrection!"

Think how Jesus could have reacted to his arrest, trial, and crucifixion. He could have come down off the cross pulled it up and thrown it down the hill at them.

Revival

The Lutherans had a revival. The first night they even tried an altar call. Old Joe, the town drunk, came forward, knelt at the rail, and prayed, "Fill me, Lord, fill me ..." and did the same thing the second night. The third night the woman next to him said, "Don't do it, Lord, he leaks!"

Rules

At a wedding reception at the Marriott Hotel in Des Moines, still dressed in clerical black, I stepped up to the free bar and ordered a glass of beer. The bartender, making a sign across his neck like a clerical collar, asked me, "Can you do that?"

Interesting how many have reduced religion to what we are not allowed to do. A set of rules.

* * *

The call came to the parsonage at 10 p.m. Holy Week. Bill Birch asked when was Lent over and Easter begun? He had counted forty days as up. Bill didn't know not to count the Sundays. I have a hunch he had given up something like beer or sex and was very anxious to resume.

Sacrifice

Marvin Kalb on NBC interviewed an old man who had the grazing rights for his cows on the land where the Pope would preside at a mass. Kalb asked, "Would the cows mind not having this grass to graze on tomorrow?" "No," was the answer, "and their milk will be all the sweeter because the Pope was here."

Sacrifice makes life richer and more worthwhile.

Saints

In September of 1997 the world lost one of its living saints. The prayer written by Mother Teresa that every Missionary of Charity says before leaving for his or her apostate, and is also used as the Physician's Prayer in Shishu Bhavan, the children's home that Mother Teresa oversaw in Calcutta, follows:

"Dear Lord, the Great Healer, I kneel before you, since every perfect gift must come from you. I pray, give skill to my hands, clear vision to my mind, kindness and meekness to my heart. Give me singleness of purpose, strength to lift up a part of the burden of my suffering fellow men, and a true realization of the suffering that is mine. Take from my heart all guile and worldliness that with the simple faith of a child, I may rely on you." — From *A Simple Heart*, by Mother Teresa, Published by Ballantine Books, 1995

Savior

At all the professional football games, behind the goalpost is a fan holding a banner which says, "John 3:16." I would someday like to sit next to that banner bearer with a sign "and 17," for it is the wonderful news Jesus is our savior, not our judge.

* * *

A sign at Saylorville Lake tells of their safety record:
  0 life lost with preservers
  18 lives lost without them
What do we have in our faith practice that can keep us afloat when all around others are sinking?

* * *

On January 13, 1982, according to Windsor and Usher of the Washington Park Police ... "It was a balding man, perhaps in his mid-fifties, with a heavy moustache and grey sideburns." He was the sixth man and he refused the rope four times for other people to take it. Air Florida Flight Number 90 had just gone down in the Potomac River.

When the helicopter went back for him he had disappeared. M.L. Skutnick, 30, an office employee of the Congressional budget office, jumped in to save a woman who let go of the rope.

We also have a Savior who rescued us and paid with his own life in doing so. To be one of the saved is quite a privilege.

* * *

Heard on National Public Radio: Mike Pearson, a conservation officer in Michigan, was called to rescue two ducks frozen in ice in a pond. He waded out, then moved on the ice with a rope. When he got there, he discovered the mallard ducks were plastic decoys. Everyone laughed at him. He said he'd do it again if called.

We ought not to be discouraged if the results of our ministries are less than spectacular. And even when we are taken in and laughed at — we'd do it again; for it's the being used for Christ and his ministry which counts.

107

* * *

An article in the *Arizona Republic* told of a two-month-old boy whose mother accidentally left him on top of her car. He fell off when the woman drove away, tumbling face down into a busy intersection.

The infant, who was strapped into a car seat, suffered some cuts and scrapes, but was not seriously injured. "The baby had abrasions to the head, but it doesn't look serious," Police Sgt. Gene Klimek said. "It looks like the baby seat really did its job."

On CNN news the story was continued to say that a semi-truck driver reported seeing the child on the road and then stopped his rig to protect it. Another had driven on by, just missing the infant by inches. The trucker was certainly that baby's savior.

Science

On HBO April 23, 1987, *Creator*: scientist Walter said, "When science does finally get the big picture and reaches over the crest, they will be surprised to see religion already there." Science often is the instrument through which God reveals how God works.

Seeing

Two hunters were road hunting in a pickup for deer in South Dakota. One was watching left, the other, right. With a sudden bang they had hit a buck standing in the middle of the road neither had seen.

There is so much we can miss that is right in front of us if we'll just take notice.

Servanthood

A special on *60 Minutes*, October 18, 1987, was about Sister Emmanuel who lives in the garbage of the city of Cairo. She claims she has "married the slums." Sixty-two years old, her theory is that you must live with the people you serve. They raised one million dollars and built a hospital. She has to fight the parents to get the children in school. One of her concerns is the women beaten by husbands she calls "beaten slaves of the garbage." This woman began life as a pampered daughter of a rich businessman.

What is it that moves some to help?

Service

At Bishop's Cafeteria there is a light on each table. When you push the button the light comes on and the table waiter knows you want service of some kind. The sign says: "For further service press button."

The light of Christ calls us to further service.

*   *   *

The women of the Lorla clan of the Kpella tribe of Liberia wanted a health center so much that they carried two building blocks at a time on their heads across the Saint Paul River in "dry time" to build the walls. It so shamed the men that they finally got busy and helped build the building. The nurse, Korlawo Togba, R.N., who trained at Lutheran Phebe Hospital in midwifery and emergency room, is the medical help for the clan. During the war of 1990 the building was burned and the men of the village were killed. The women and children ran to escape into the bush. How brutal we humans can be to each other!

Sign

David Brenner on the Johnny Carson show told about signs he never quite understood:

1) The International House of Pancakes on their door: "We have menus in braille."
2) A New York restaurant was even better: "For bathrooms, use the stairs."

What signs with mixed messages do we give out to people who see us practice our discipleship?

*   *   *

Another sign — this one at Broadlawns Hospital: "If you are pregnant, inform the technologist."

Sin

I was following a car down Harding Road today and read on it a bumper sticker: "To know me is to love me." Just as I finished reading it, someone inside rolled down the window and threw out a bunch of paper trash and garbage from Burger King. We imperfect sinners are not all that lovable when people get to know us!

* * *

Told by Gerhard Forde: A Baptist told a Lutheran, "The trouble with Lutherans is they never get any better." The Lutheran replied, "We are just honest enough to admit it." So it is with our theology which describes us as we really are: sinners and saints.

* * *

Rodney Dangerfield does his comedy monologue by interspersing the profound comment: "It ain't easy being me." It's true, because we do not get better and better, we remain very imperfect. It's not easy living our lives and with other sinners also.

* * *

Andy Rooney on *60 Minutes* claimed no one is to blame for anything in our country. "... the good boy got in bad company; it was the pusher's fault not the drugtaker; the person was legally insane at the time of the crime." He ended by saying, "Don't blame me for what I just said. The devil made me do it." Christians can own their behavior and seek forgiveness but often still have to pay the price of it.

* * *

Elmo Zumwalt III in Vietnam was exposed to Agent Orange which his own father, Admiral Zumwalt, had ordered to be sprayed. Elmo III's son was born with a birth defect. Elmo has cancer. The admiral has had a bone marrow transplant and is "... doing okay for now."

"The sins of the father upon...."

* * *

A bridegroom was arrested after allegedly shooting his new wife in the stomach soon after their front porch wedding, authorities said. Luarette Kenny, 38, and Raymond Brunson, 50, apparently got into a fight as the reception wound down. She pitched a plate of macaroni salad at him and then got shot with a .22-caliber handgun, police said. Friends said things seemed to be going fine and they weren't sure what happened. — *Oakland Tribune*, April 18, 1992.

Life goes sour even with the highest motives.

*   *   *

In March of 1987 the media announced that the Rev. Jim Bakker of PTL Club fame had been caught having sexual relations with a secretary, Jessica Hahn. Tammy Faye is in an institution for drug addiction. William Simbro, religion editor of the Des Moines paper, called and asked if the church could take yet another scandal like this! No human can take excessive public scrutiny! It is always dangerous to worship the personality (cult) as flawed as we all are!

*   *   *

I went to the optometrist. I learned a blind spot in my vision is where the optic nerve is. So I took a Humphrey peripheral vision test, punching a button when a dot appears.

We certainly all have our own blind spots, recognized or not, about ourselves or others or circumstances.

*   *   *

Dan Rather announced on CBS nightly news on March 31, 1987, that the AIDS virus "resurrects itself." Kill it and it somehow starts again. So the bad can resurrect as well as the good! Addictions, prejudices, bad habits, greed, and so forth.

*   *   *

At the marriage of Bob Harker and Julie Davel the father of the bride lit the unity candle during picture taking and it broke in two. I picked it up and got hot wax on Julie's hand. Sometimes there is pain in being unified.

*   *   *

The grass in the yards is all brown now for lack of rain, but weeds are thriving from the cracks in the concrete. Interesting how

111

the good often seems to wilt away in very favorable places and the unwanted seems to thrive where we don't want it to survive.

* * *

On a Northwest Airlines plane they place a plastic cover over the engine intake while loading the food from a truck to the plane's galley.

I wonder what we ought to cover and with what to keep from contaminating our intake which propels us through life?

* * *

We came upon the scene of an accident at Big O Tire Store in Pittsburg, California. We could see the corner of the building marked from missing the curve, skid marks on the street, anti-freeze stain from a ruptured radiator, pieces of chrome and glass on the street. Sunglasses and a blood-stained cap, shrubs broken down, and an inside of a headlamp were there. An accident had happened. How often we see the signs of the accidents of people's lives. Can we who are Christ's find a way to prevent them and give comfort to those to whom they happen?

* * *

In the 65th anniversary of the Grand Ole Opry there was a monologue telling of country western "hurting songs." When Willie Nelson got the prize he was called one who composed and sang "close to the ground."

Perhaps "hurting songs" reflect how painful our sinful lives are. I wonder if our preaching and ministries are close enough to the ground.

* * *

In the movie *Out of Africa* Dennis said to his lover, "Mapmakers, when they got to the edge of where they knew, would write: 'Beyond this place there be "dragons!" ' "

A good description of beyond the church. Luther described in "A Mighty Fortress" "waiting to devour us."

*   *   *

The palm tree outside my office window on the seminary campus must have the dead fronds removed every so often so new ones will grow. The Christian life does call for the removal of the dead that new might grow. Let's see, what ought we remove?

prejudices	old enemies
wealth addiction	saved-up hurts
selfishness	jealousy

*   *   *

In the movie *The Crying Game*, the captive says to the captor of the Irish Republican Army, "There is a story of a frog and a scorpion. The frog carries the scorpion across a river on its back. Halfway across the scorpion stings the frog and the frog asks why. The scorpion replies, 'Because it's my nature.' "

Our nature is to sting rather than to love. Only with God's help can we change.

*   *   *

ChemLawn did the church lawn today and left a note to tell me they had given it a "pre-emergence treatment for crabgrass." Is there such a pre-emergence treatment to prevent greed, wealth addiction, selfishness, racial hatred, adultery, and all the other sins which destroy our lives?

Singing

Our message as congregations is often garbled. The little girl came home and announced she had learned: "Hail Mary, full of grapes," and then they sang: "Where shepherds washed their socks by night."

Spirit

In *The San Francisco Chronicle*: "Pepper Spray Stuns Oakland Congregation." A sixty-year-old woman was hospitalized and twenty other Oakland churchgoers were treated for eye and throat irritation after a pepper spray canister accidentally went off inside a woman's purse. It was at the Green Pasture Church. According to

113

the newspaper, "The fumes spread, causing some church members to develop symptoms." — March 18, 1996.

What might be the symptoms of the spirit's being set free? Apostolic radical, infectious witness syndrome, greed appendicitis, grace co-dependency, servanthood obsessive-compulsive, and so forth?

*   *   *

Cherry-colored Maalox "for all your Maalox moments."

How about prayer and God's presence for all our difficult moments?

Tums advertises extra strong which are "... twice as strong and twice as fast" for those times when you need extra help.

*   *   *

A commentator on a television program titled *Save the Planet* said, "Every country has three kinds of wealth: 1) material; 2) cultural; 3) biological." Could we add spiritual, or lack of it?

*   *   *

Don Strong in explaining preventative maintenance said: "We should be proactive rather than reactive. You don't wait till something breaks before you replace it." So, too, with our spiritual faith. We must work at it before the crises of life threaten to break it.

*   *   *

My asthma is especially bad today. I breathe but get little effect from doing so. I think it can be so in the church as well. The Spirit's wind of Pentecost blows but we get very little effect from it.

*   *   *

A recent newspaper account of a fire in San Francisco stated the fire department is looking for "suspected accelerants in the ashes." How about Pentecost accelerants? What is it the spirit of God can best use to accelerate the Pentecost fire again? Let it be us through whom a new fire is ignited in the souls of our people.

Oh, that we could accelerate the fire in our soul to witness, steward, minister to, and have compassion for all God's people.

*   *   *

Nissan cars have an ad on television I like a lot. The old farmer looks at this dilapidated pick-up and says: "She's been good to us, but I reckon it's time I go into town and get a new one." He returns driving wildly into the barnyard doing doughnuts and shouting with glee as he drives his new Nissan. His wife asks, "Wilfred, what's got into you?" He answers, "I don't know, but I like it!" Oh, that we might celebrate Christian joy and let the spirit get in us. The promise is, we'll like it. "Life is a journey, enjoy the ride."

Spiritual Life

I was buying chemicals for use in our hot tub when the woman asked if I wanted a fragrance. I asked which one smells religious? She smelled three before realizing it was a joke. How does religion smell? Can you smell kindness, mercy, gentleness, forgiveness, humbleness, precious love?

*   *   *

Carved on a Danish church pulpit near Grand View College in Des Moines, Iowa: "Blessed are the people who have an ear for the sound from above."

Let us never be deaf to God's speaking.

*   *   *

Champion Batteries has an ad on television. The Mister leaves the lights on all night. His wife is due to have a baby. She comes out of house to go to the hospital. He gets in and the car won't start. She opens the hood and flips the special booster switch which starts it and off they go.

Our booster is always ready to help.

*   *   *

I visited the Wolfsens' ranch in Central Valley at Los Banos, California. They were preparing a new field for growing tomatoes

115

by using a large road grader which was controlled by an infrared beam. This beam moved the blade up and down so that the field would be exactly the level which made irrigation possible.

Perhaps the saints have given us a measure for our spiritual lives like that.

There are also infrared beams for our practice of discipleship: Bible, other good lives, preaching, confessions of the church.

*　　*　　*

I saw the movie *Awakenings*. The setting is a hospital in the Bronx. A Dr. Sayers experimented with these people who seemed alive inside but in a trance outside. It was an experiment in drug therapy. These patients had awakenings which let them come back for a while.

Can we bring awakenings in our spiritual lives gone dead on the outside? Memories of first communion, confirmation, youth groups, and so forth, that awaken in us the near presence of God.

*　　*　　*

In an awful movie titled *King Ralph,* Ralph asked, "What you do all day is not nearly as important as what you are." Yes! The older I get, the more I am convinced it's *being* that really counts. Much more than *doing.*

*　　*　　*

Some things I noticed while serving as chaplain on a Caribbean cruise over Christmas:

There is a man who stands on the bridge and watches ahead — in addition to the sailor steering the ship.

The lines are first taken to shore by a small dinghy with little ropes — then the large ones pulled in.

To dock, water jets propel the ship sideways.

Everyone takes part in a lifeboat drill the first night aboard.

Jugglers tried to do their floor show during heavy seas.

I could feel the boat moving two days after getting off the ship.

They put a harbor pilot on the ship each time they come to a different harbor.

There are cabin stewards, deck stewards, and so forth.

*   *   *

Dr. James Karol prescribed sulfa each day after my surgery for prostate cancer. The sulfa was to ward off any infection before it got started. This is called prophylatic medicine. It prevents trouble before you are in trouble.

How might we administer or prescribe spiritual prophylatic ministry? Prayer, regular worship, study of the scripture, and spiritual direction would be a start.

*   *   *

I now have a pill box with compartments for each day of the week to make sure I get the correct medication each day and remember to take it each day.

In our religious lives we need to have certain things regularly in order to stay spiritually healthy: prayer, forgiveness of others, thankfulness to God, witness to others.

*   *   *

We had to have the tires on our Ford Explorer rotated today after 20,999 miles. We had to reverse and turn over our mattress as well. Are there spiritual rotations we need to do, like new prayer life, new ways of worship, new hymns, new preaching which will enliven our spiritual lives like fluffing up an old pillow?

*   *   *

According to the famous attorney, Gerry Spence from Wyoming, on *60 Minutes*: A young smart aleck tried to fool a wise old man with a little bird in his closed fist. He asked the man, "Is the bird alive or dead?" If the old man said, "Alive," he would crush it. If he said, "Dead," he would let it loose to fly. The old man answered, "The bird is in your hand."

We often have the privilege and awesome responsibility of taking life or nurturing it. The bird is in our hand, also.

117

* * *

HMO's are everywhere — health maintenance organizations. We who are God's church are SMO's — spiritual maintenance organizations. Annual check-up, regular devotions, test the heart for capacity! What ought we do to fulfill our God-given mandate?

* * *

On each airplane flight I take, the flight attendant announces in similar fashion: "In case of emergency, put on your oxygen mask first, then help the child next to you." We must develop our own spiritual lives first in order to help those around us.

* * *

I saw today on Highway 80 a lead car in front of a very big earth-moving machine being transported on a "lowboy" truck. The lead car had an antenna to check the height of the overpasses and was hooked up by radio to the driver of the lowboy.

We need be warned often of the need for centering so we can clear the numerous threats to our spiritual and physical lives.

* * *

I was at a busy intersection in Des Moines (Harding and Hickman) when a brand-new red fire engine came up the street, siren blaring. An older woman did not hear the siren and pulled out in front of the engine. It put on its brakes, burned rubber, and stopped. The sudden braking killed the engine and now it would not start. Finally some of us from the filling station pushed it over to the side. The battery was worn down trying to restart the motor. Meanwhile the lady in the Chevy went on down the street.

We can have the finest equipment, but to no avail if we don't keep the battery charged. So too our spiritual lives ... and what havoc we wreak in the lives of others without ever even knowing it.

Stewardship

Bill Moyers on CBS news talked of the United States Congress overriding sanctions on Central America. He said Congress was being "the stewards of the nation's conscience."

We Christians must claim the task of being stewards of the nation's conscience.

* * *

Dick Peterman told a story of a pastor who stayed in the same parish for fifty years. It was in Pennsylvania. His first wedding was the daughter of a wealthy coal mine owner. The father gave the pastor a gift of a pair of kid gloves which he didn't use. Fifty years later at retirement, the pastor tried on the gloves and found a ten dollar bill in each finger, given to him during the depression when that was a lot of money. For fifty years he didn't use his gift.

Identifying and using our gifts to the best use is the essence of stewardship.

* * *

On the January 28, 1988, television show *Night Court:* Bull is hit with lightning and thinks God tells him to give everything to the poor. Actually Art, the maintenance man, over a walkie-talkie was saying to Bull who was helping mount a television antenna: "Give it everything and pull."

In the last scene, after Bull has given everything away and finally finds out it was Art speaking, God comes to him and Bull says, "But I have the joy of giving to others and that's the way we get close to you — by giving away. Thanks, God." God replies, "You are welcome. Sorry about the polyester underwear."

Giving is one of the great secrets of the good life.

* * *

I saw on CNN news that a man had won six million dollars in the state lottery. He told all he would do with the money, including spoiling his grandchildren. His wife said he forgot to buy her a valentine this year. The first time in forty years of marriage! He had bought a recreation vehicle that weekend and was out driving it around.

How easily wealth can help us change our priorities.

*   *   *

What a story on *NBC Nightly News*! It was about Russian and American troops in prisoner of war camps. Americans would receive Red Cross packages and share them with Russians at risk of death. The Russians would not tell the guard when a prisoner died but would hold up their body in line so as to get their food allowance.

We are without risk and the saints' bodies are held up that we might feast on their food.

*   *   *

Corinne Chilstrom wrote to me to tell of using a story about Doris Bergman. The choir director at a rehearsal said to Doris, "Doris, I think there is a solo in there!" And there was! He convinced her to sing and it was lovely and many congregations have been blessed since by that fresh, young choir director's *gift identification*.

*   *   *

Dorothy Day is supposed to have said: "If we render unto God what is God's, there will be damn little left for Caesar."

A therapist at LSS: "You can be right or have a relationship."

*   *   *

An article in *USA TODAY*: "McThief Probe"

"A customer at the Euclid, Ohio, McDonald's drive-up window was mistakenly handed the day's cash receipts. The company sometimes conceals the 'take' for the day in one of their regular paper bags to foil thieves. The person receiving the bag of money may not have committed any crime according to the authorities."

God drops undeserved gifts on us, too.

*   *   *

William Sloane Coffin said that there are two ways to be rich: "One is to have a lot of money; another is to have few needs."

120

Our culture foists on us so many false needs for which we sacrifice too much.

*   *   *

Andy Rooney on *60 Minutes*: "There are more people on the earth alive right now than have ever lived and died here. If God would rewrite the Old Testament now, instead of 'be fruitful and multiply,' God would say: 'enough already!' "

I believe Andy is correct and that family planning has become crucial to our Christian stewardship.

*   *   *

A sign in the Sizzler Steak House in Albany said, "No sharing. Please, do not put us in an awkward position."

What is awkward for that restaurant is surely basic for discipleship.

*   *   *

In the days of old, when a king converted to Christianity and ordered his knights to be baptized, many of them held their right arms out of the water. As they were submerged into the baptismal water, they kept their weapons dry so they could continue to use them in ways of killing and war. I sometimes have a picture of us modern Christians undergoing our baptisms while trying to hold our wallets and purses out of the converting waters. — The deaf Episcopalian.

*   *   *

In Shakespeare's *Romeo and Juliet* performed at Orinda, California, Juliet says to Romeo, "The more love I give to thee, the more I have." There it is again — we give it away and it most affects us.

*   *   *

In a play I saw in Chicago the woman says, "Right now I have in me the power to create another human being. When I think about

121

that I think of myself in a whole different way. I wonder if God felt that way when God created me?"

The potential to create new life is awesome and calls for a special stewardship of life itself.

*   *   *

Andy Rooney on *60 Minutes* told a story of a woman who looked out the window of a commuter train and saw one of her gloves. So she pulled down the window and threw out the other glove so there would be a pair for someone. We have quick and passing opportunities to be unselfish. It doesn't come very naturally but God calls us to that kind of lifestyle.

*   *   *

It was a long breakfast line at the pastors' retreat. Some came to the "traveler" toaster and took their slices of toast without putting in new bread. Soon there were no slices and all had to wait.

Stewardship is providing for those who will come after you. Upon taking your toast, you place new slices in the toaster for those farther back in line.

*   *   *

Johnny Carson on *The Tonight Show* tried to kid about the possibility of a nuclear war. He said the only one to survive would be Ted Koppel, who "remained to do the wrap-up."

We must take seriously the stewardship of having the capacity and equipment in place to wipe out the human race.

Carl Sagan says he thinks we have been sleepwalking in this country for thirty years on this subject. Many biologists believe it will be the extinction of the human race.

Where are the theologians to speak on this issue? We must speak and pray and act.

*   *   *

At the TWA flight counter, they have a box you can use to test the size of your carry-on baggage, so you can determine if it will fit under the seat.

I'm wondering about a gauge of some kind you could use to test the size of your offering. Perhaps it could be in the narthex and you could put your offering envelope or billfold or purse in it. After all, it's the proportion of what we have been blessed with that is what God would have us share. We give not so much because the church needs it as we give because we have a big, big need to give it away.

*   *   *

An employee of the church who had been stealing from the offering was caught by using a powder which showed up red on the hands of the culprit when placed under a special light. There are many ways we steal from the church and park the getaway cars in the church parking lot. Giving much less than a tithe of our income to Christ and the church would certainly be one of the ways.

*   *   *

A sign in the restroom of an American Airlines plane: "As a courtesy to the next passenger after you, may we suggest you use your towel to wipe off the basin." A basic tenet of Christian stewardship is to consider the effect of our lives on the people who come after us. It could be called resource inheritance.

*   *   *

A scene from television's *Night Court* which really moved me: Bull has fallen in love with a hooker who is milking him for his money. When he finally realizes it, he says, "I feel sorry for you. I see many like you. They take and take but they can't give because they are empty in there and they can't get filled." I wonder what the writer of the show had in mind as he or she wrote this great message of stewardship.

*   *   *

Life on the farm always had unwritten rules I observed, followed, and assumed everyone did. Whenever Grace Miller, the neighbor, baked, she would send over a pie for us. I always had the task of returning the pie pan to the Millers. My mother always filled it with something like cookies when she sent it back — never an empty pan. And when my father borrowed a tool like a mower, we always cleaned and oiled it before I drove our Model A Ford to tow it back.

That's the way it ought to be in our practice of stewardship. We return a little of all which has been given us.

* * *

When taking camp counselors on canoeing and camping trips into the provincial forest of Canada, we learned of the law of the woods. Under a lean-to there would be some dry firewood ready for starting a fire. And we were to prepare the same for the next camper.

It's a principle of Christian stewardship. We always carefully consider those who will come after us as we consume the resources of now.

* * *

A small town was trying to raise money to bring the big city symphony to their high school gymnasium for a concert. One ticket seller went in to Joe's barbershop. Joe said he would be out of town and was sorry he could not be there ... "but I'll be there in spirit." The ticket seller responded, "And would you like your spirit to be in the $12 or $15 seats?"

It's a matter of stewardship to put our money where our spirit wants to be.

* * *

The newspaper article simply stated, "Orphan found jewelry, becomes rich this week." A sixteen-year-old orphan found a vinyl bag by the railroad tracks near his home in Hollywood, Florida, and thought it contained costume jewelry. Now he has found out the 116 pieces are worth about $400,000 to $600,000. The boy's lawyer said Eric has dropped out of school partly because of the publicity over the find. Our lives do have underestimated treasures yet to be discovered. Also, riches can destroy our best of motivations.

*　*　*

Douglas John Hall writes regarding stewardship: "Stewardship does not describe any one dimension of the Christian life, it describes the whole posture called Christian. The stewardship of all believers — stewardship is the church's mission."

*　*　*

I preached this Sunday morning at Saint Luke's, Phebe, Liberia. An old ordained deacon presided at the service. At the time for the offering, a woman brought forward a pan of peanuts on her head and placed it at the altar. Another brought a bucket of corn. These were the first of their harvest and they were literally offering them to God as their "first fruits offering"; then, the following week they could harvest the rest of the crop for themselves. Here was the biblical "first fruits offering" in practice!

Suffering

When flying into Stapleton Airport this morning, we took a very bad jolt. The pilot explained this as being caused by "jet wash," which came from a plane which crossed our path a while back and we could not now see two miles to the left of us.

We get "bumped" by the jet wash of others, their good or poor actions before us. A former pastor, lover, employee, family member. When it jolts us, it is a surprise. Being able to understand this can help us adjust to the rough flying conditions.

*　*　*

In 1991 *Newsweek* did a story on economic hard times. The following were three responses in the letters to the editor:

"It takes an enormous amount of gall for the administration to try to solve the problems of others when our own country is going down the drain."

"What next — serfs and peasants?"

"Hard times," wrote one, "free us to discover what we truly value in life."

It was the same situation seen by different people. I don't believe God gives us hard times so we learn from them; but God surely helps us make the best result out of our hard times.

*   *   *

On flight number 981 (United Airlines), there were storm clouds all around the horizon. The captain announced, "Fasten your seat belts, because we do have some turbulence even in the friendly skies."

It's true even as God's people and in God's care there are storms and rough roads to travel.

*   *   *

Close to Des Moines, a fire was reported north of Ames, Iowa, and close to Fort Dodge. A satellite spotted it even before it was reported to the local fire department. From way up in the heavens trouble was seen even before those on earth nearby took notice of it.

God in the heavens knows our troubles and wants to help.

Thanksgiving

Tom Brokaw, on the Thanksgiving evening news, said, "When we sing the dirges, we must also sing the anthem." He went on to say we must recognize not only the miseries of life but also the joys. So it is being a sinner and living in an imperfect world.

Time

The National Technical Information Service announced in 1997 that the average U.S. citizen spent his time this way:

— 1,595 hours watching television, or just under 4.4 hours a day.
— 2.9 hours a day listening to the radio.
— 45 minutes a day listening to recorded music.
— 27 minutes a day reading a newspaper.
— 17 minutes a day reading books.
— 14 minutes a day reading magazines.

I wonder what is the average time spent in prayer and worship. Or how about the number of hours spent in serving others?

126

Tradition

Reverend Richard Perry told the Iowa Synod in assembly about a man cutting off the end of a ham before putting it in the oven to bake. When asked why he did that, he said because his mother always did. When she was asked, she said, "My grandmother always did." When she was asked, she said it was because she didn't have a pan long enough for the ham!

Custom and traditions in the church are like that. Once they start, we carry them on without asking their significance.

Treasure

A thief cut out of an alarmed frame a $175,000 Monet painting from Fisher Community Center in Marshalltown, Iowa (March 19, 1987). No one noticed that the treasure was gone for a while. We, too, can lose the treasure and not know it.

*   *   *

The newscaster recently told of an owner of a jewelry store putting a bag of diamonds worth $175,000 on top of his car and driving off to the airport. They have not been found yet. It's so easy to lose our treasure and sometimes not even know it for a while.

*   *   *

Dr. Scott Kinnes was a critical care specialist in Oahu, Hawaii, until he went to a garage sale about two blocks from his home. There were trash bags stuffed with old papers, photos of movie stars, and autographs obtained by the Zanes sisters who worked at the San Francisco Opera House and the Curran Theater. Some of the autographed photos included Clark Gable, Charlie Chaplin, Laurel and Hardy, Mary Pickford, Vivian Leigh, Carole Lombard, Orson Welles, Errol Flynn, Duke Ellington, and Louis Armstrong plus some Presidents of the U.S. Kinnes paid less than $10,000 for all of it. The surviving sister "wanted to get rid of the stuff." It had been gathered over forty years. It is now valued at more that one million dollars. Kinnes said, "I feel obligated to go back and give them a bonus now."

We often don't recognize the value of what we already have.

*   *   *

This is absolutely fascinating! At the DeSoto Missouri Valley National Refuge there is a steamboat recently discovered in the earth at least one to two miles from where the Missouri River runs. Over the years the river has changed course and is now a couple of miles away. This boat was completely covered and found recently.

What other treasures are just below the surface and are waiting for us as we dig deeper into real genuine existence?

*   *   *

In January of 1998 we explored Superstition Mountain, Apache Junction, and Goldfield City east of Mesa, Arizona. We learned of an old Dutchman who came to Apache Junction. Every so often he would go out to Superstition Mountain and return with fine gold. He died without ever telling anyone where the mine was. People by the thousands for many, many years have searched for the infamous Lost Dutchman Mine.

Estee Conaster wrote a book, *The Sterling Legend,* about the Dutchman and his mine. He claimed there are three main theories about the mine.

1) Apaches had hidden and closed up its entrance so white men would not return to their mountain.

2) There had been five Mexican mines. The Mexicans had hidden their take and were killed in the Mexican-American War and the Dutchman had found this cache which was not a mine at all.

3) An earthquake and landslide had completely covered the entrance to the Dutchman's mine.

There is still a store in Apache Junction which sells mining machinery and supplies called "Pro Mac." There are also clubs which go out regularly today still trying to find the Dutchman's gold.

Truth

Winston Churchill is supposed to have said once about his potential opponent: "Baldwin occasionally stumbles across the truth. But he picks himself up and goes on without any notice." — Karl Langrock at a Grand View College Board of Directors meeting.

TV Commercial

A couple quotations: "We measure success one investor at a time." — Dean Witter. "A pledge and a promise" — Anheuser-Busch. "You can get there from here" — Shearson-Lehman.

* * *

Coke has an ad in which one of the workers at the Olympics stands up on the winners' platform, hands clasped over his head in a sign of victory. He acts like he can hear the absent crowd roar approval.

* * *

An ad for Contac says: "Until there is a cure, there is Contac." We could say that about loneliness, guilt, sin — until there is a cure, there is the cross; until there is a cure, there is communion.

We are victorious also. In Christ we have won over death, sin, and the power which works against God.

* * *

Ads for cars are interesting.

Toyota claims: "Every day belongs to you, make it count." A good stewardship of life itself. Every day we have been given to minister on God's behalf. Let's make it count.

Saturn says: "A different kind of company, a different kind of car." Let our congregations be able, with God's help, to say the same thing. Not a service club or country club — as nice as they are — but a different kind of company, one which follows the Christ and ministers on his behalf and celebrates his presence with us now.

Cadillac touts: "Live without limits," as if that is a happy way to enjoy our lives. Not really. A disciplined life lived carefully

129

and consistently with Christ's example is where real joy will be found.

Victory

At Bethlehem Lutheran Church in Oakland where I preached today, there is a mentally challenged older man whom they helped learn to usher, receive offering, do communion. His name is Buddy. After he finally had received the offering and handed it to the acolyte, in exuberance Buddy raised his two joined hands in the air like a champion.

We have won! We are God's champions — for Christ has accomplished our victory. Raise your arms in victory and celebration.

*   *   *

Going through white water rapids is quite an experience! When we went through the roughest one of all, part way through, we lost our rudder and then our guide fell in. Some fell into the center of the rubber raft and some fell out into the river. Finally came the calm water and I thought we had made it, only to discover all were gone. I was on the raft alone! The guide and all the passengers had been dumped. I think we often experience that kind of disaster in the wake of our hollow victories.

Violence

In the movie *Witness* Grandpa tells his grandson Samuel, "What you take into your hand, you take into your heart," as the boy takes a gun into his hands. We can ask what we put in others' hands and what our hands seek to hold.

Witness

Mercedes Benz has an ad on television in which a big, new, black Mercedes crashes into a wall for research on safety. When asked why they share the scientific information with other auto manufacturers worldwide, the researcher responds, "Because some things in life are too good not to share." So, too, the gospel — just "too good not to share."

130

In Shakespeare's play *Antony and Cleopatra* the messenger tells Anthony, "The nature of bad news infects the teller." And so too of the good news. Reason enough to preach! In order that the preacher might more strongly believe and the witness be effective.

*   *   *

In Iowa the highway snowplow trucks have two mirrors on them. One is on each side of the rotating blue light so you get the effect of three emergency lights rather than the one it really is.

We can be the mirror of the light of Christ in the dark world in which we live. We are not the Christ, but we are called to reflect him.

*   *   *

In the musical *Evita*, Eva Peron said of herself: "I am content to be the woman who brought the people to Juan Peron."

I am content to be known as one who brought the people to Jesus.

*   *   *

Dick at Our Primary Purpose, an AA treatment center: "I don't lecture; I just tell them how it was with me being drug-dependent." They understood and wanted that same help. Dick said to them, "I don't have to be alone anymore."

So Christians' interpersonal witness: we don't lecture. We just tell them about our relationship with God. And the more we witness, the more we own the gospel, and we don't have to be alone anymore either.

*   *   *

In an interview with the director of the Diakonia Werks, Herr Schoenhaus, I learned that 1,400 mentally challenged and old and sick were bused out of Neuendettelsau to the gas chambers. At another of its institutions the director refused to let them be taken, but here they cooperated and they were killed during the Third Reich. In times of some moral crises we may have a chance to take a stand, but often it seems more reasonable to capitulate with the strong powers which work against God.

*   *   *

It was during the great snowstorm of 1973 when Mansfield, Ohio, was covered with many feet of snow. James Truley drove his truck into a snowbank and became completely covered. He survived by eating snow in the cab of his truck. His brother came to Mansfield looking for him and found the truck on State Route 13 inside the city limits after several days. I met Truley at the trauma center and he told how sheriff's deputies and National Guard went right over the top of him without knowing it. Finally the airport snowblower uncovered his truck. The lost was found. How many are still in the cold waiting for our discipleship to uncover them?

*   *   *

It is told of the "Swedish Nightingale," Jenny Lind, that she always spent a few minutes alone in her dressing room before giving a concert. She would strike a clear vibrant note and then pray, "Master, let me sing true tonight." Might our prayer be similar. Let our witness sing clear and true.

*   *   *

At a men's retreat I was presenting on discipleship, I made my usual plea for disciples to witness to their faith not only for the purpose of bringing others to the gospel, but also for the effect that witnessing has on the person who does the witnessing. For the more we witness, the stronger we believe and the better we become at witnessing and the more certain is our ownership of the gospel.

After the lecture David Lindberg, a retired faculty member of the Lutheran Seminary at Chicago, reminded me of how it was for Greek actors years ago. They all wore masks to represent whatever character they were playing. It is said, according to David, that wearing the mask not only affected the audience, but also had a profound affect on the actor who wore it. Looking out the eyeholes of the mask, the actor saw the audience's reaction to the mask and so was shaped even more into the part he was playing. So, the

132

gospel does change and shape us as we relate it to another person. Reason enough for a witnessing congregation.

Worship

In *The Covenant Book of Worship* published by Covenant Press in 1981 (p. 11): "The rhythm which emerges in Biblical worship moves between memory and anticipation. Its integrity lies in its backward look of faith, its forward gaze of hope, and its present response of love."

Now that's worship.

* * *

The Chicago Ozark Airlines made the following announcement: "Freedom Airlines is now beginning the final boredom process." Sometimes our worship and preaching get so routine and humdrum we could begin with a similar announcement: "The final boredom process."

* * *

The pastor was ill in the hospital and the congregation worried about her. Several messages that week went to the janitor to fix the bulletin board for next Sunday.

The supply pastor said the hymn title would be: "God is good."

The church secretary said to put on the outside board that the pastor is improving in the hospital. So the board read:

"God is good.

The pastor is better."

Sometimes we worship the pastor rather than God we serve.